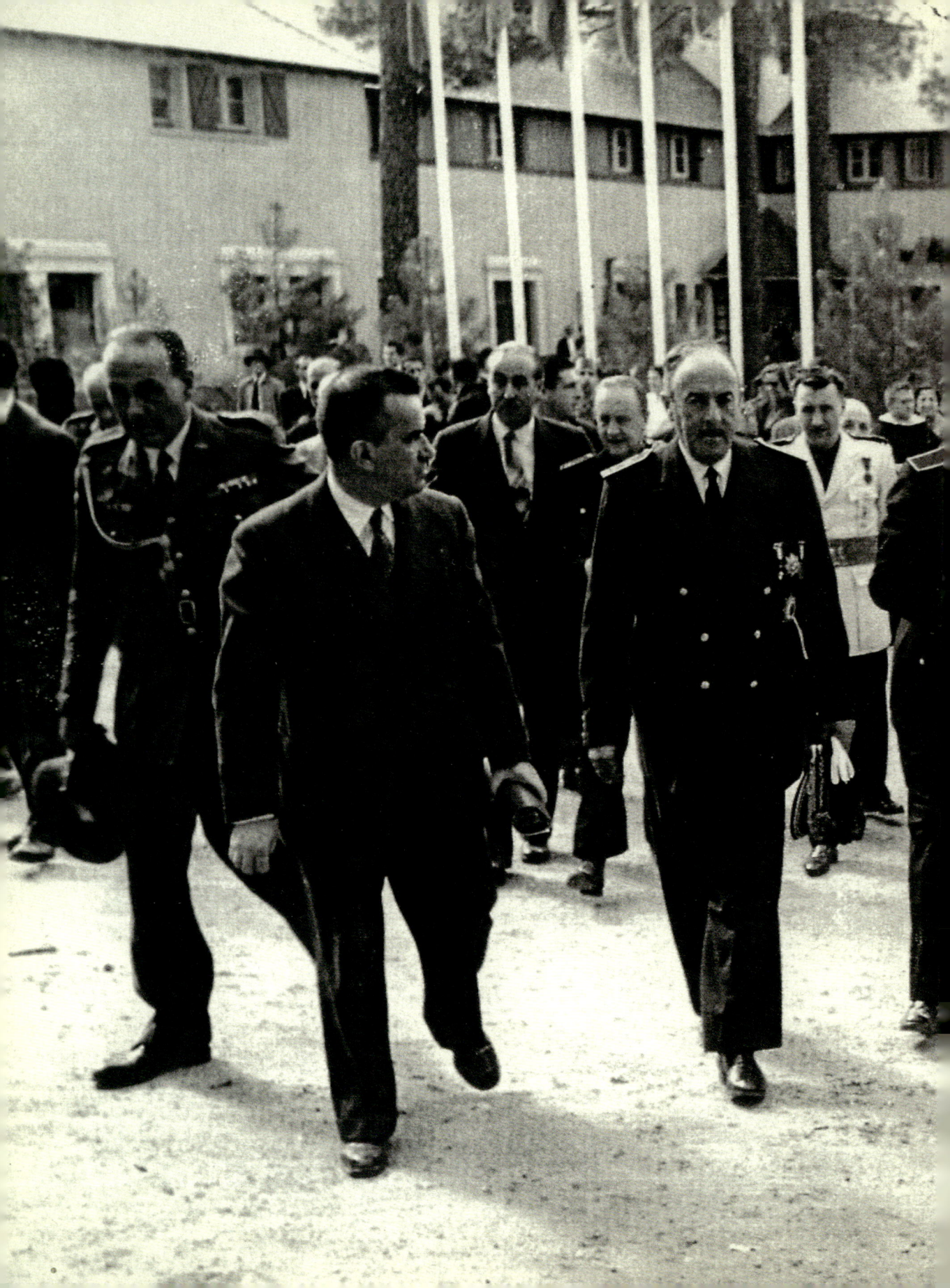

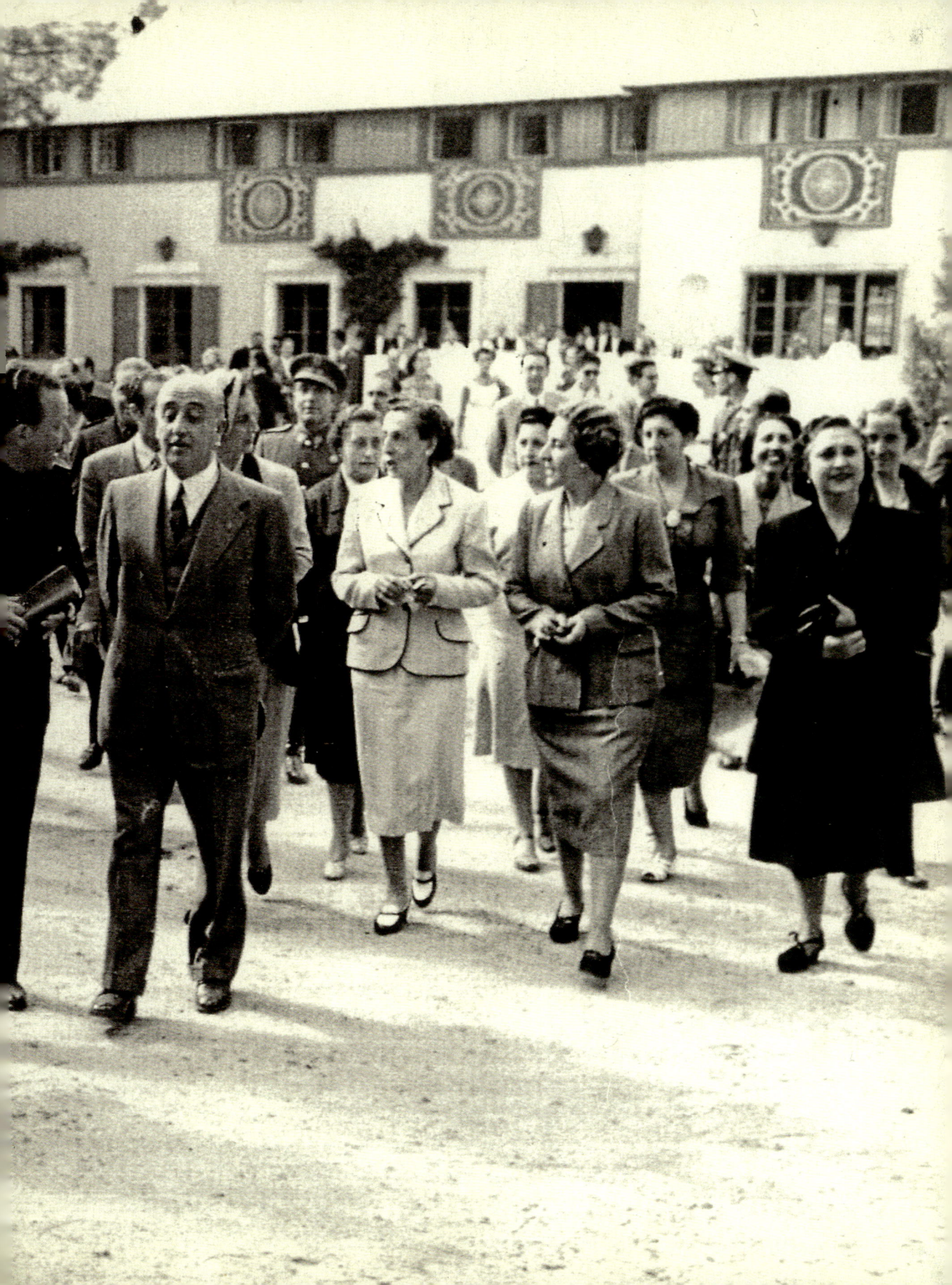

for my beautiful
friend Brette

warm hug
(un abbraccio tenero!)

but Beautiful

Cristina Nuñez

Le caillou bleu

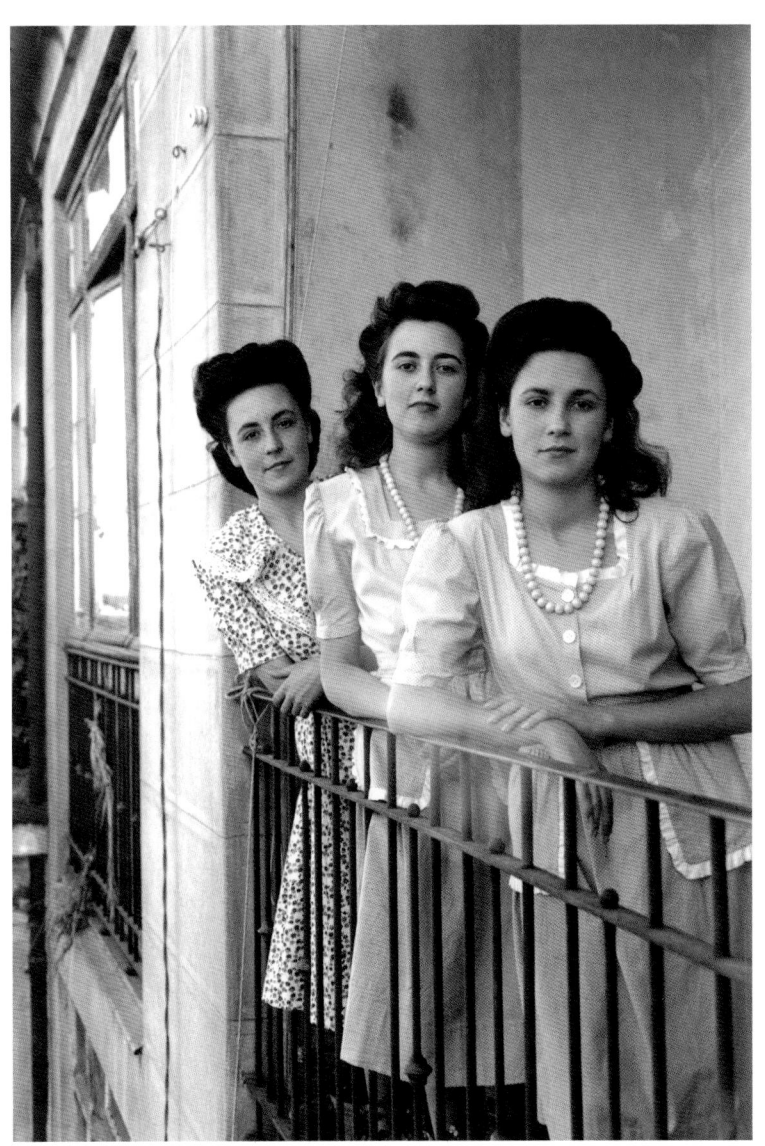

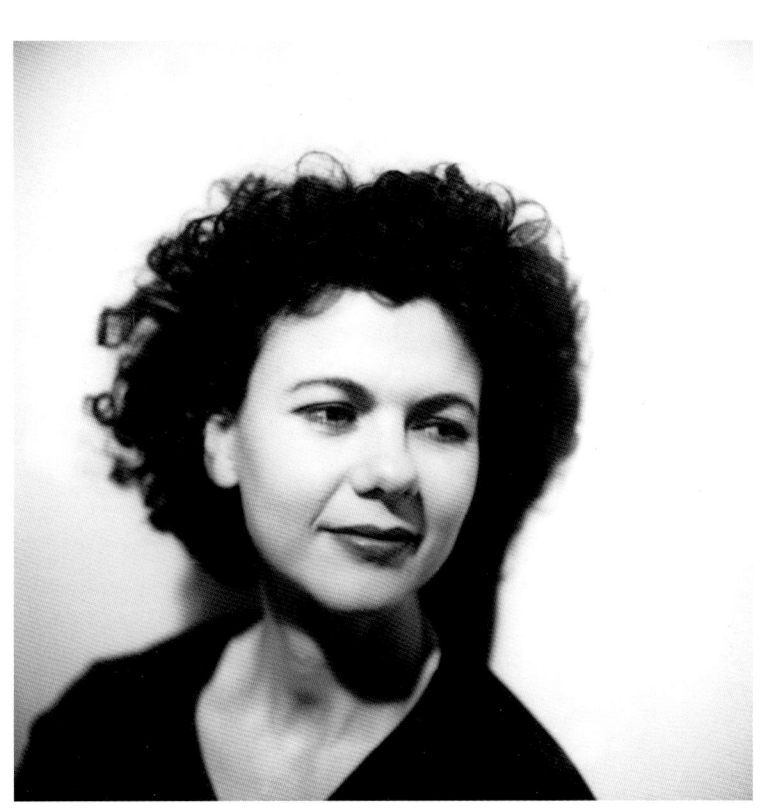

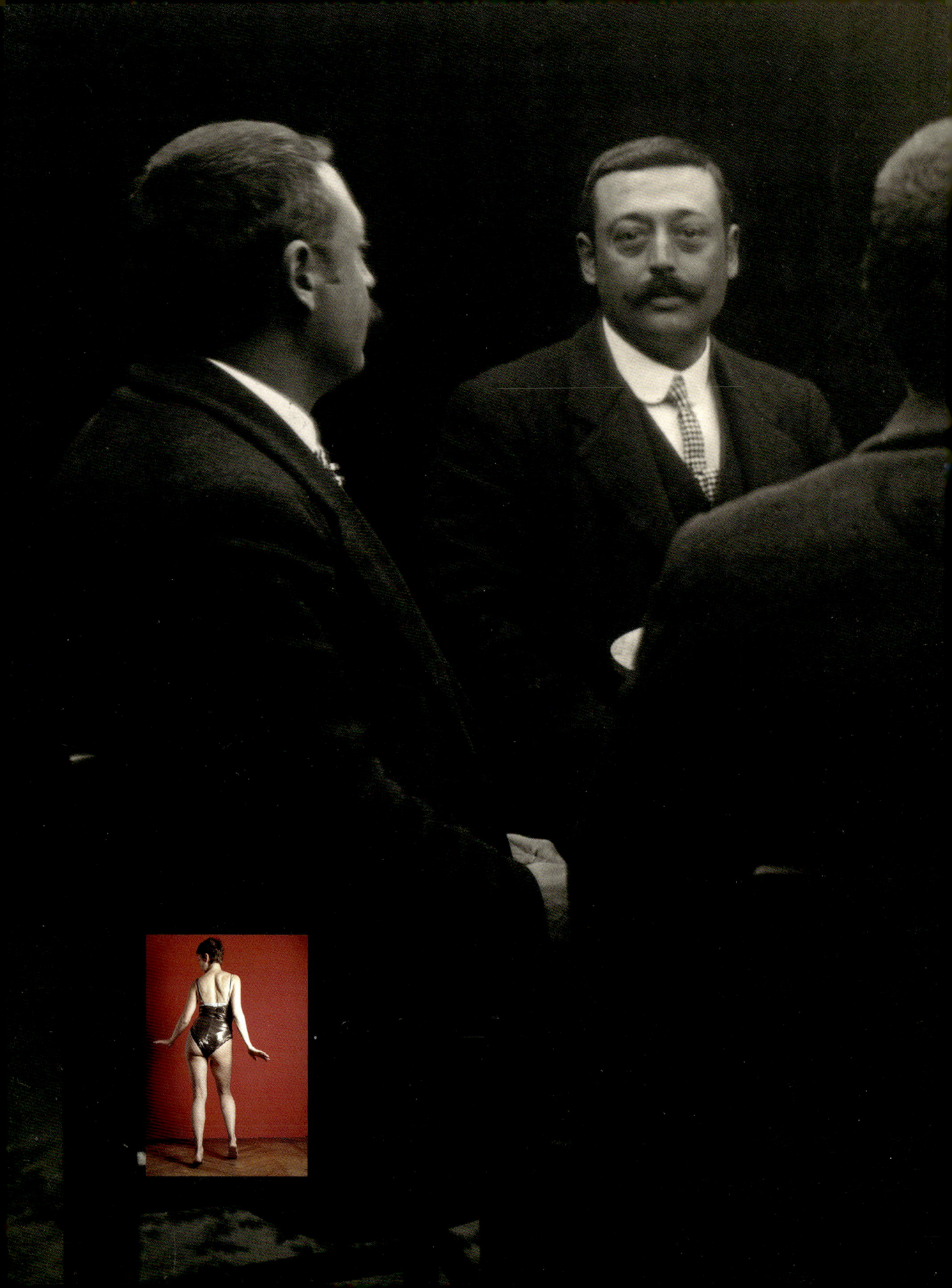

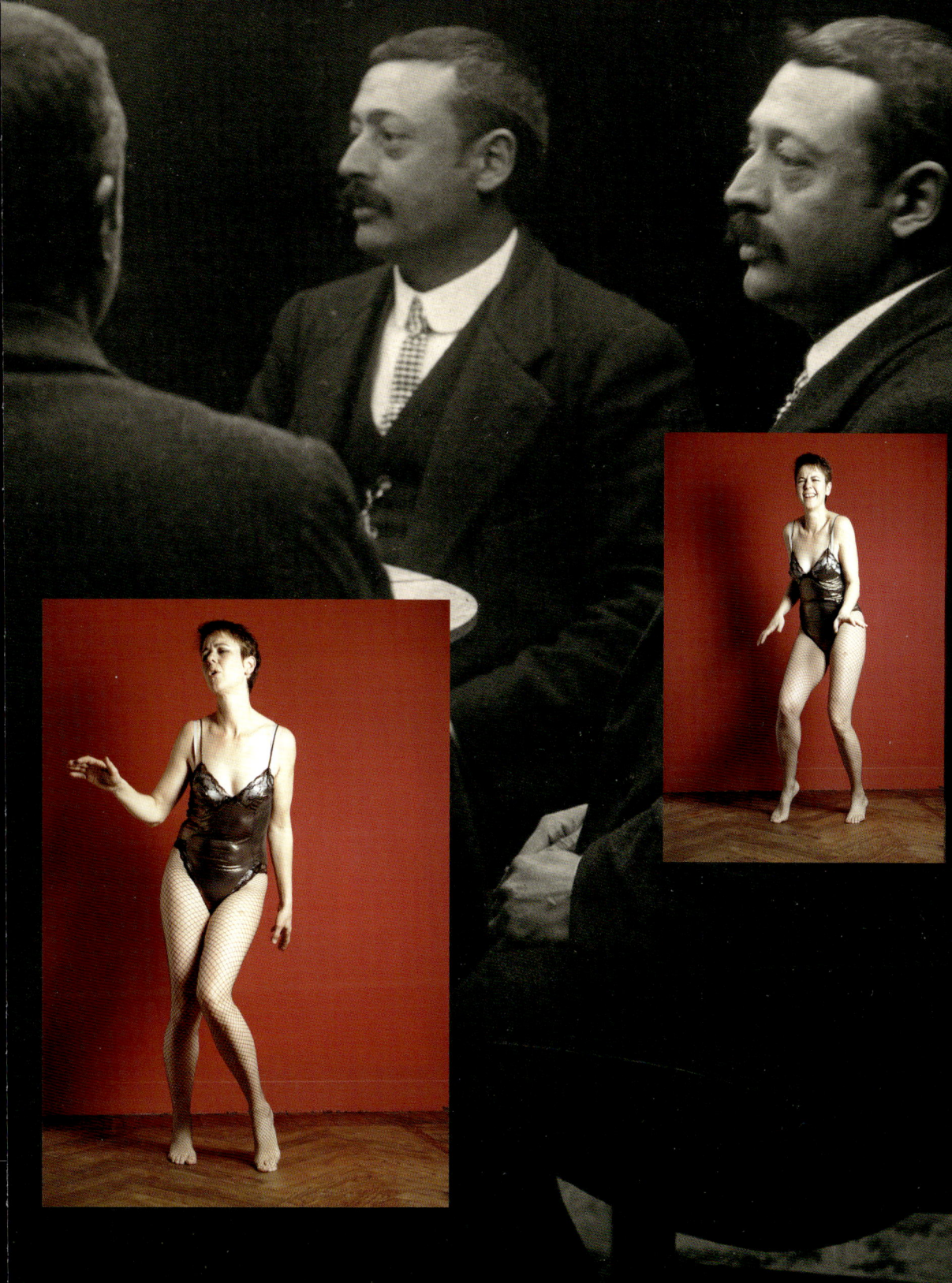

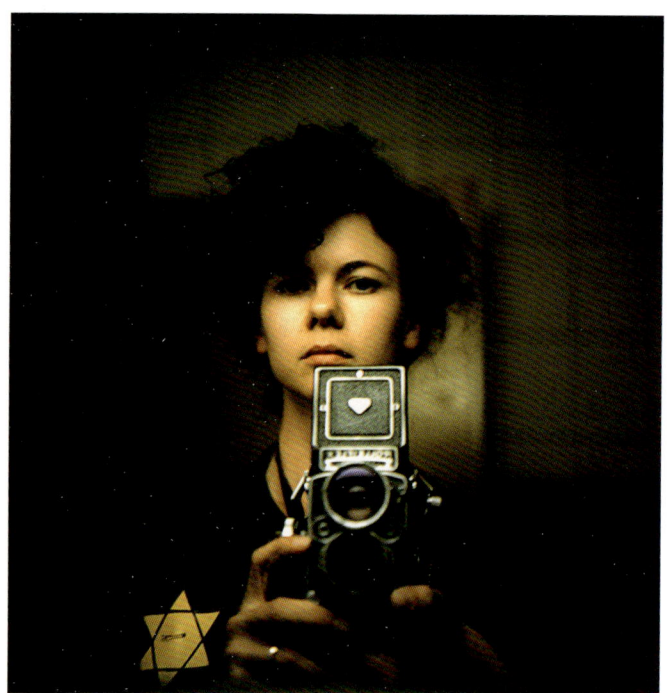

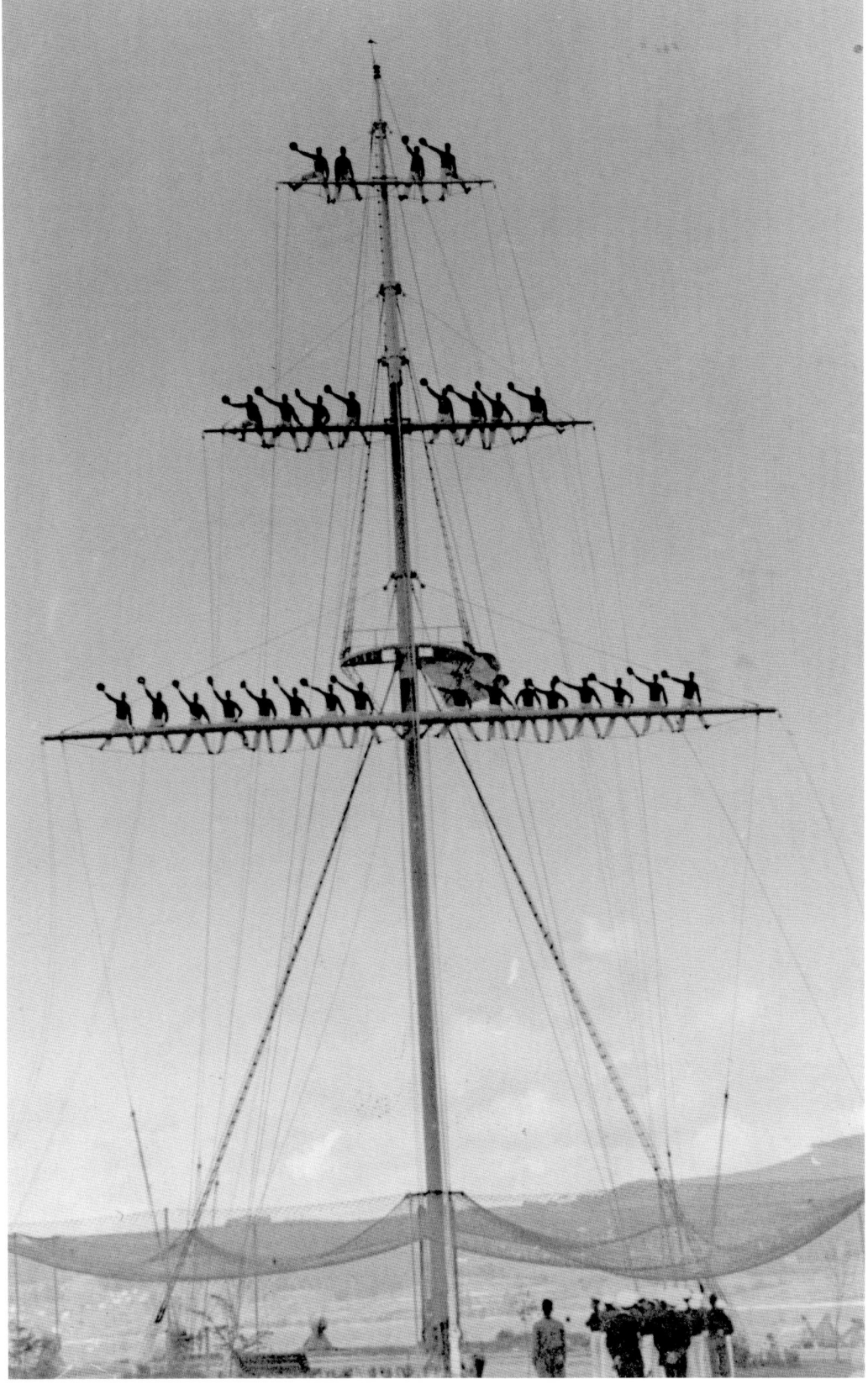

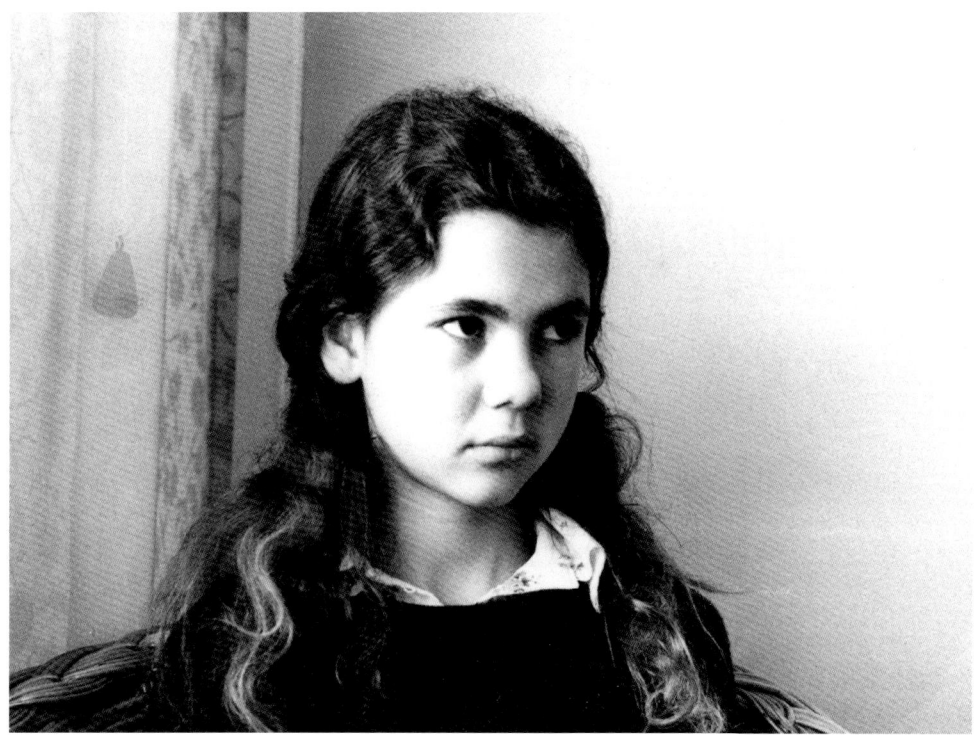

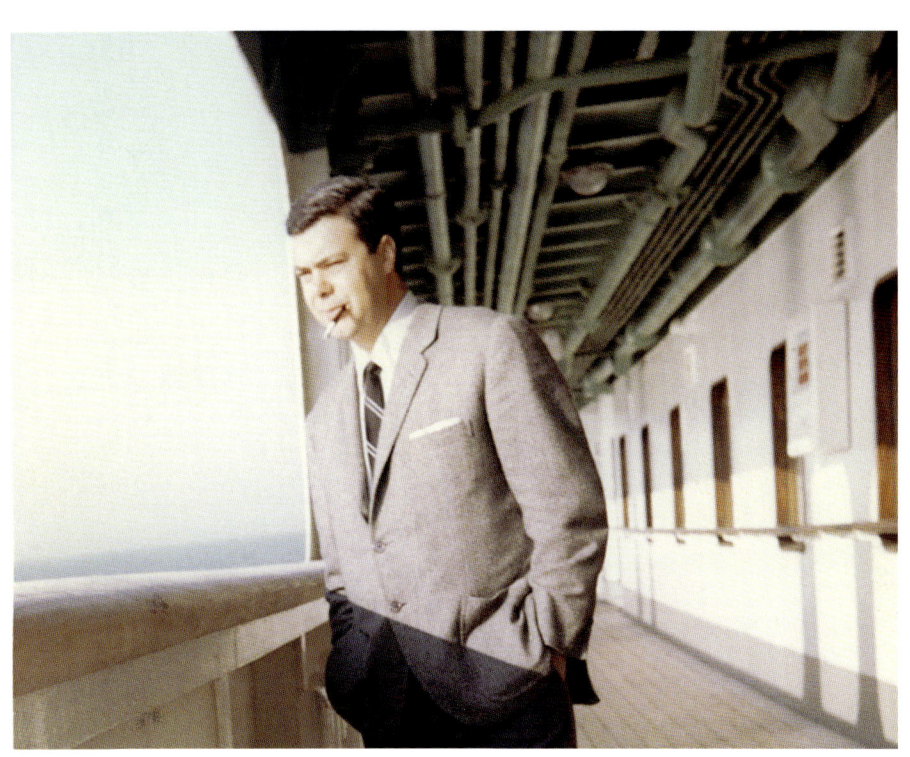

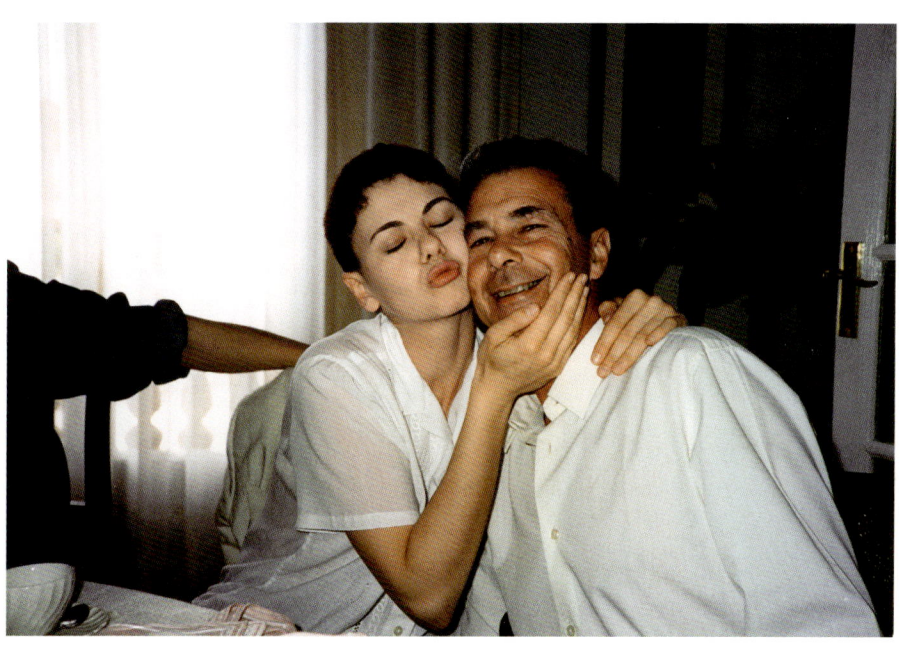

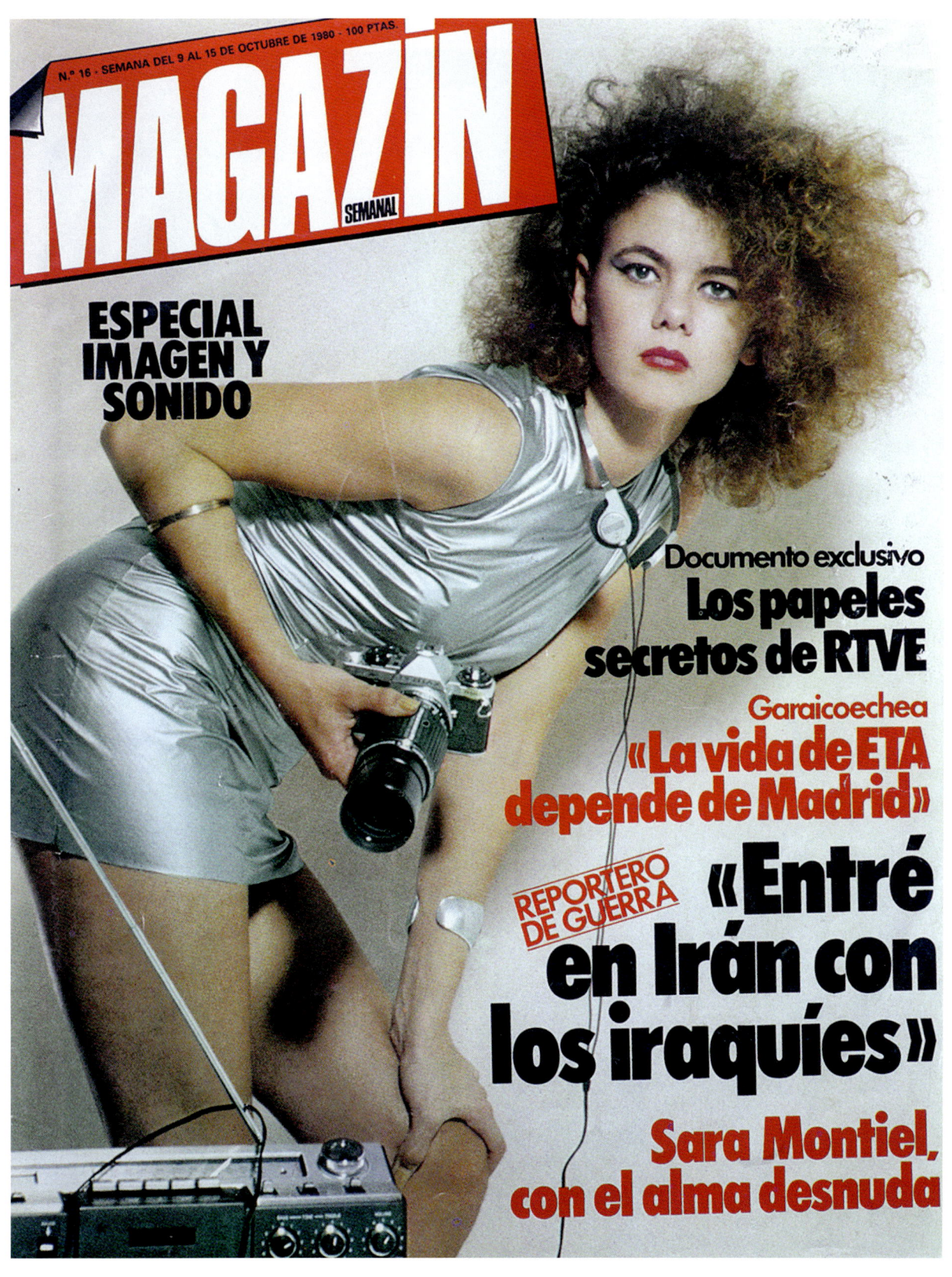

N.º 16 · SEMANA DEL 9 AL 15 DE OCTUBRE DE 1980 · 100 PTAS.

MAGAZIN

SEMANAL

ESPECIAL
IMAGEN Y
SONIDO

Documento exclusivo
Los papeles secretos de RTVE

Garaicoechea
«La vida de ETA depende de Madrid»

REPORTERO DE GUERRA
«Entré en Irán con los iraquíes»

Sara Montiel, con el alma desnuda

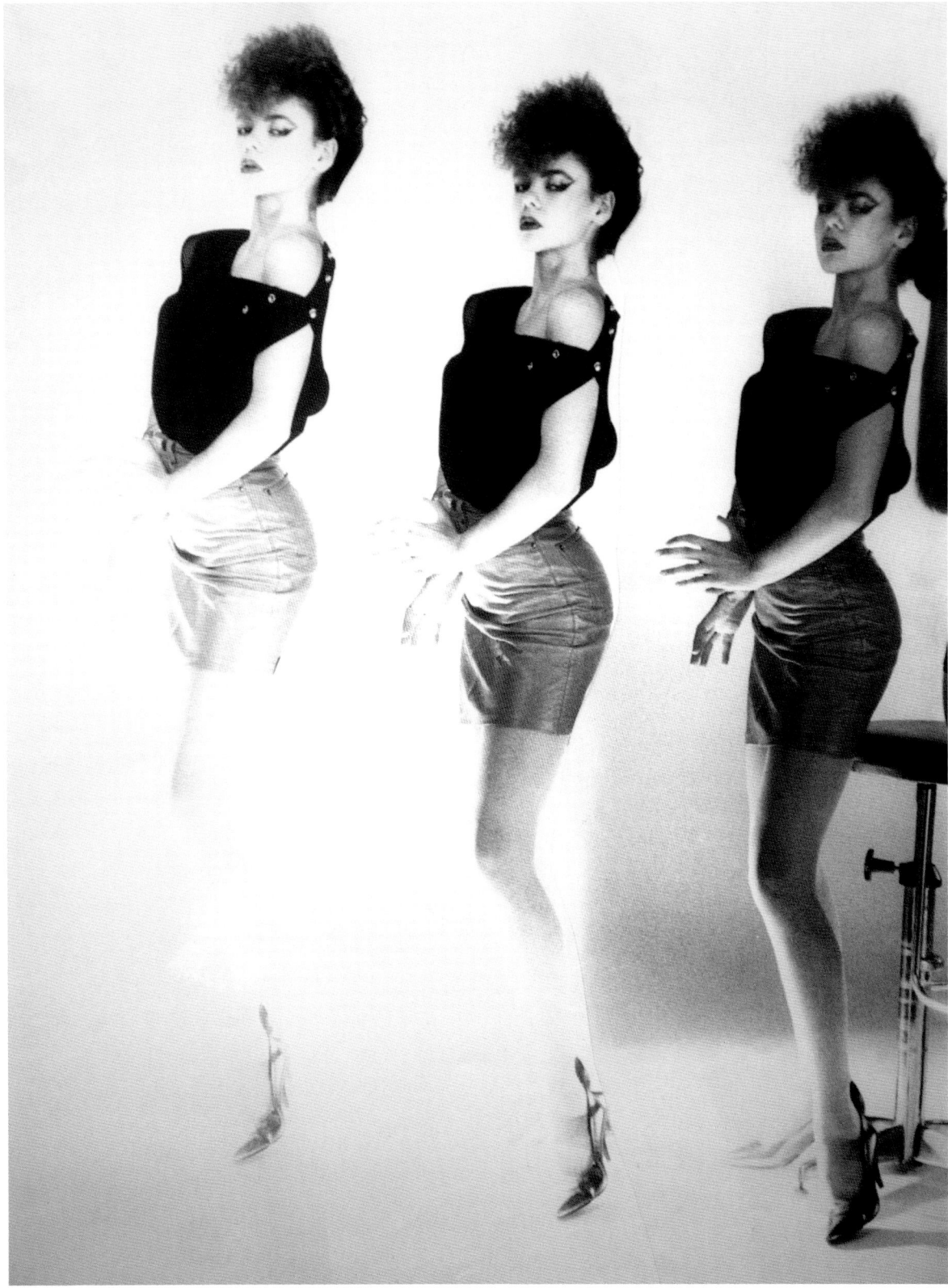

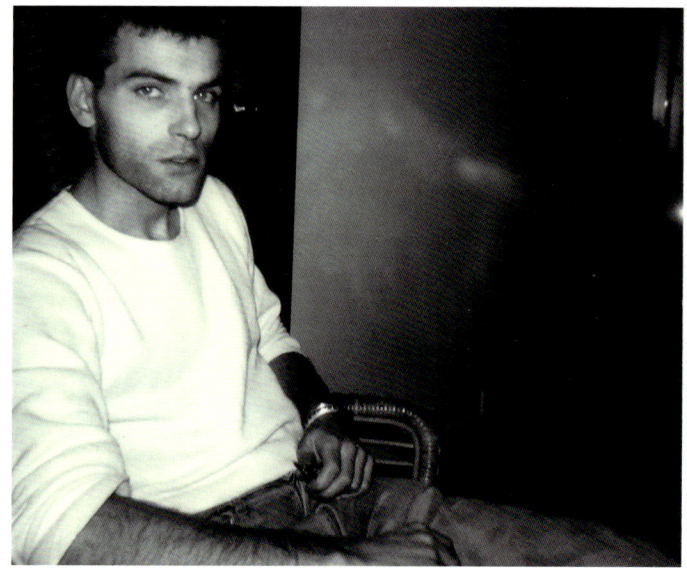

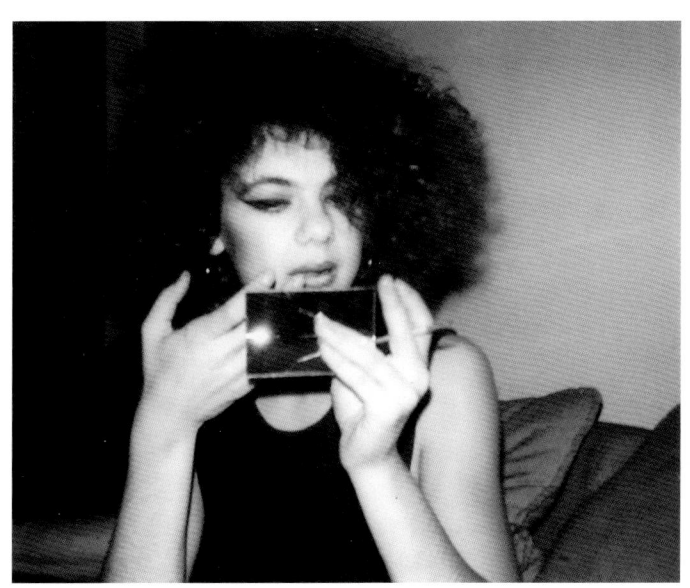

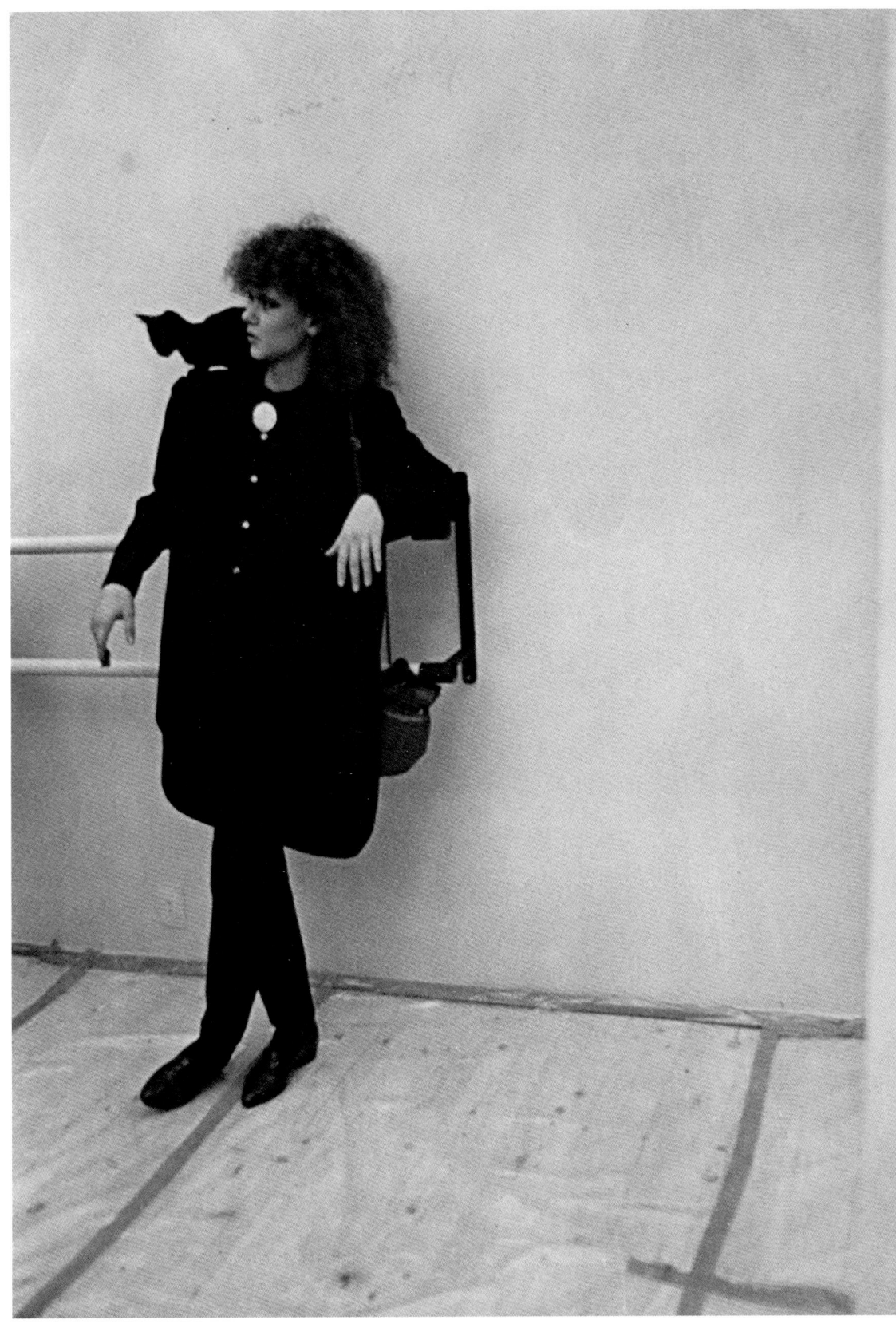

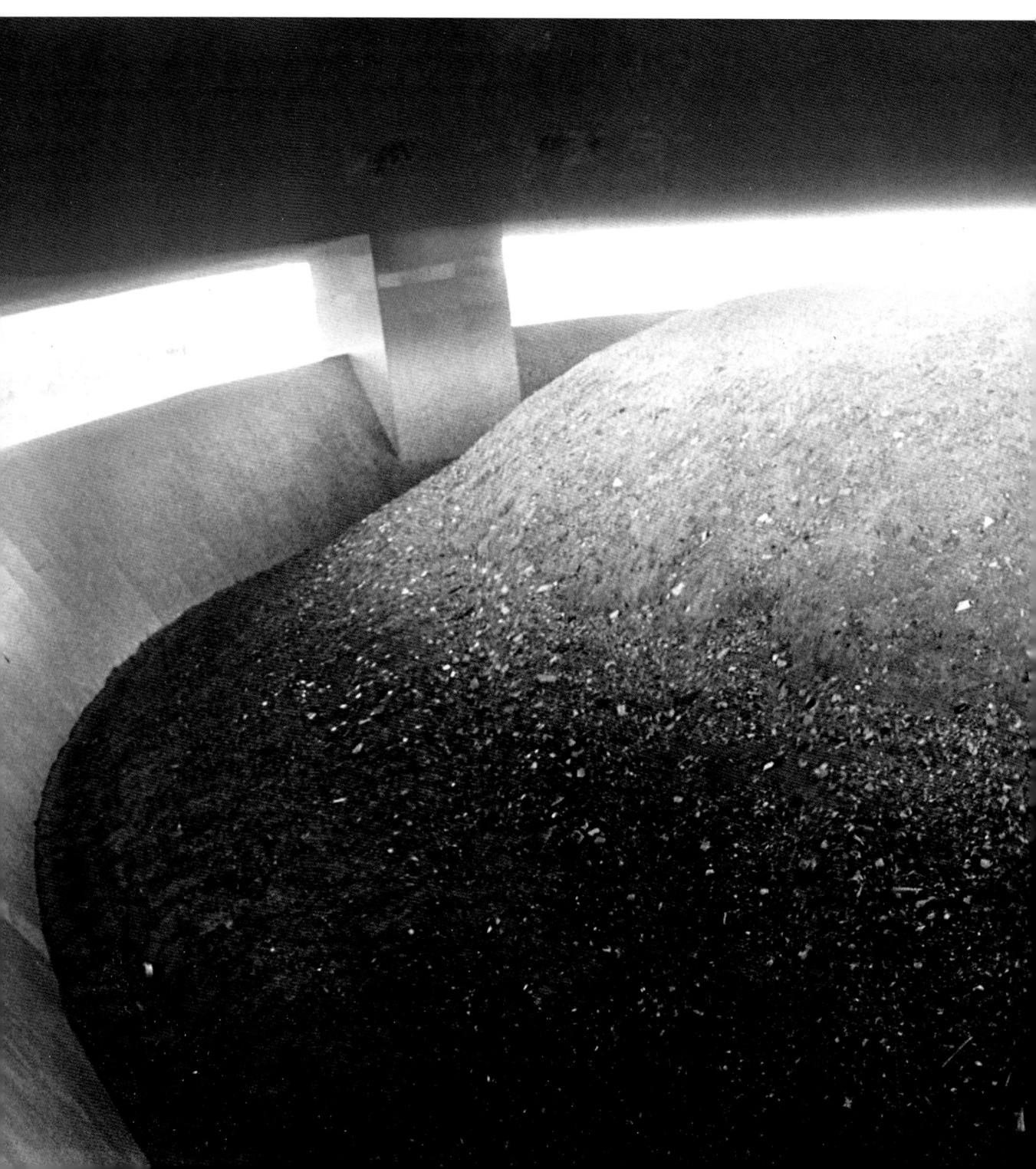

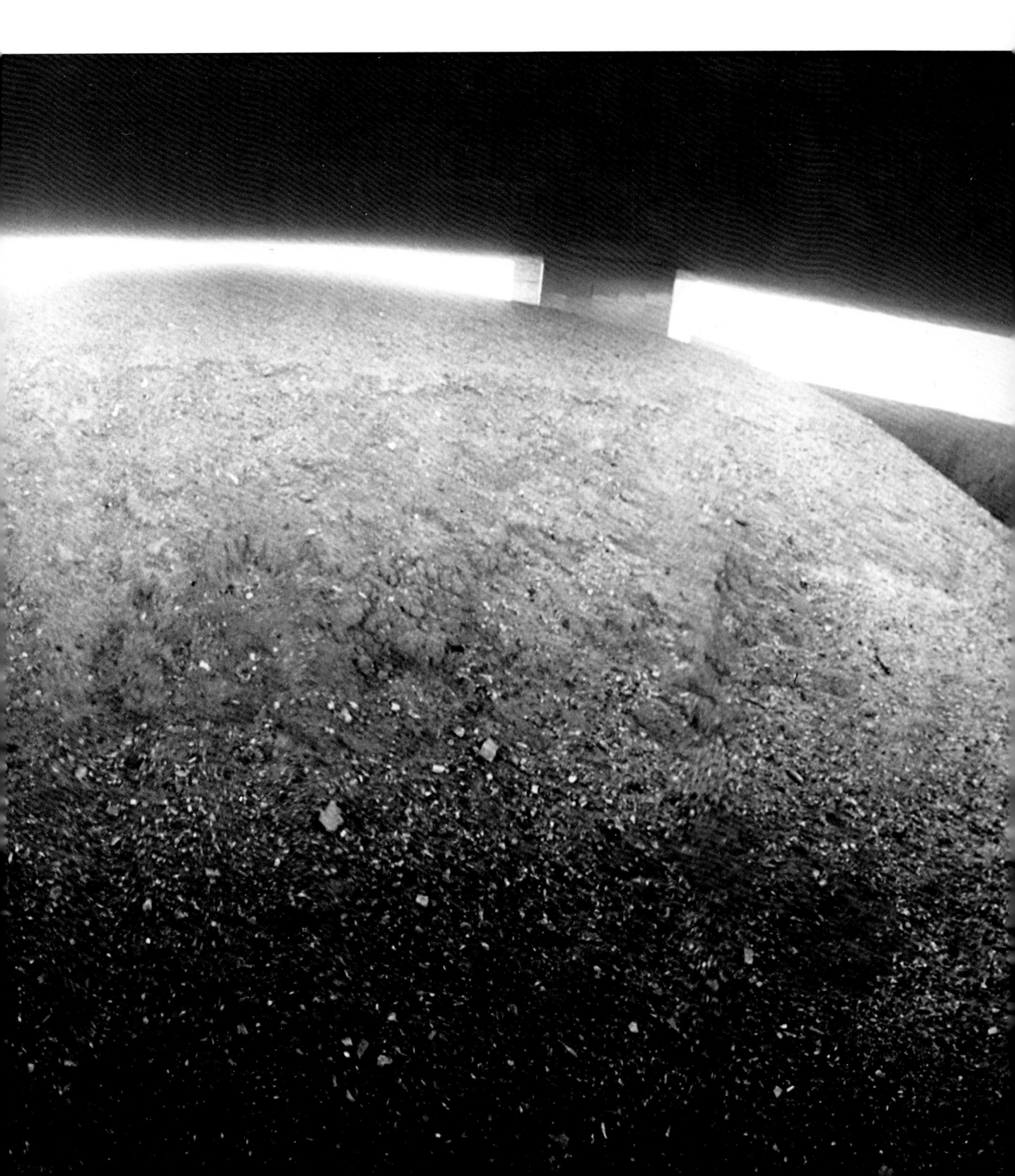

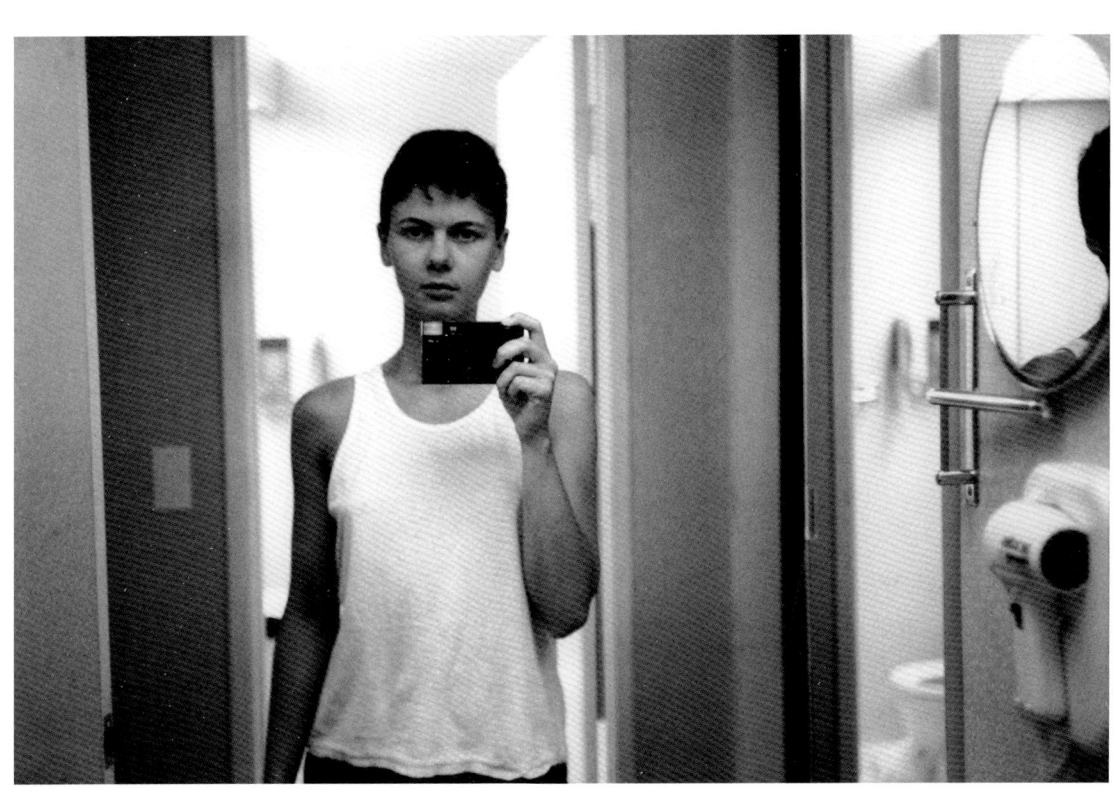

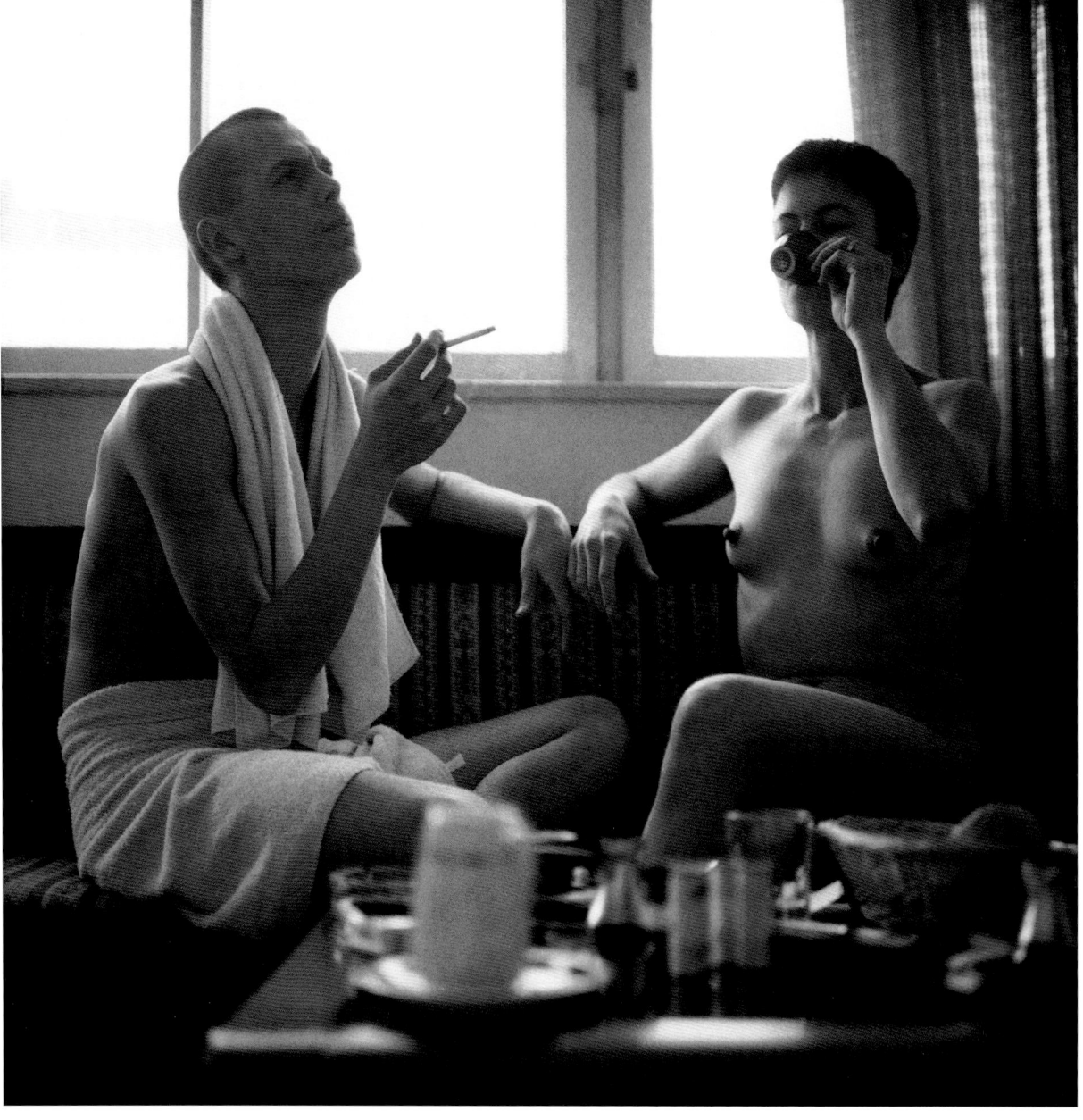

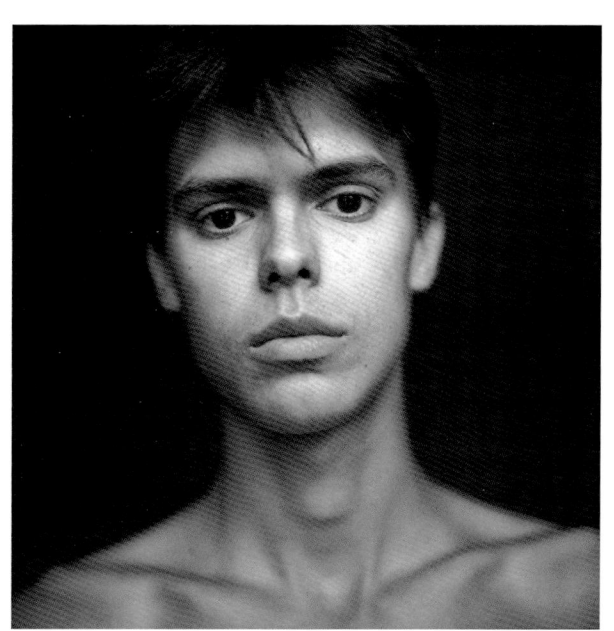

My dear Cris, just today I recived your parcel and I belive that nothing ever made me so happy as this carton box! Literaly! Well it is even verry dificult to write this letter to you as I am so excited. Because of the informations I got, because of the tape of ML. wich I find excelent, and I am sorry we never had chance to realy play and create together, he is good, and real and tell him that I wish him and his Bianka and his wife all the joy and I wish him to stay good. Now again about you. You are so great and beautifull as your realy are Real RODES OF GRACE and aldo we are separated and our lifes are some how diferent we are one and we are the same. I think I never was more close to anybody on this world, you made me mad, and gentle and crazy and sane, and everithing posibly I was and I will ever be, you made me to be me and I am gratefull, now you support me and take care of me like a beautifull sel of love and every drop of your sea is life to me, Yes I love you, and I will always love you no mutter what. That love made me go mad, make me scream and shout as I am not next to you to take care about you. I've been tieing to forghet, to run away, and than you came back to my life, and I welcomed you. I will always welcome LOVE and give love, we are love, I love you, love you, love you, love you. Maybe Army made me understand and I am sorry if this make some

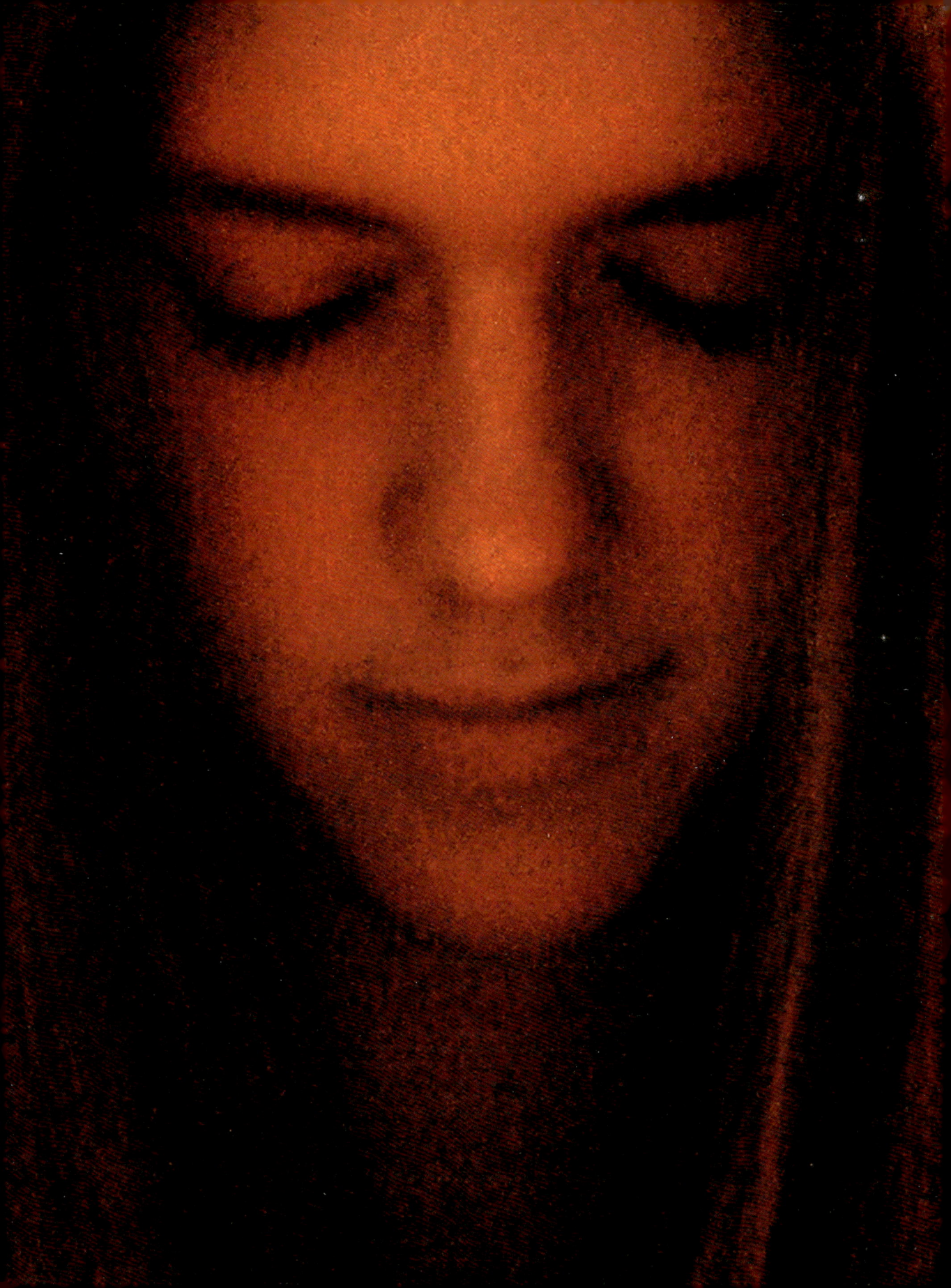

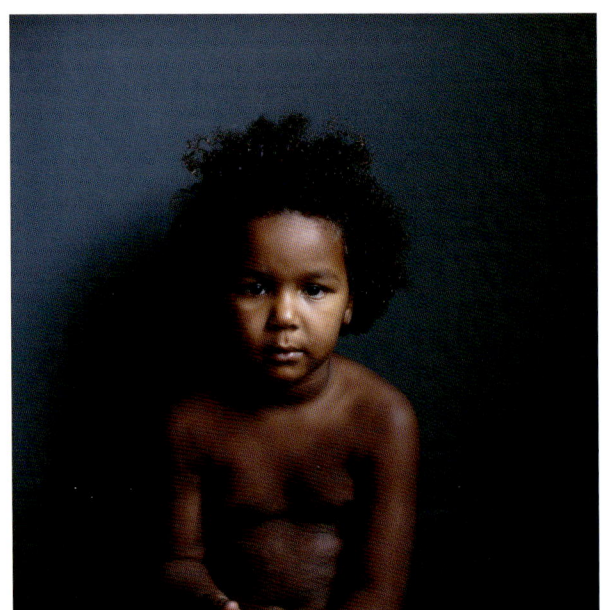

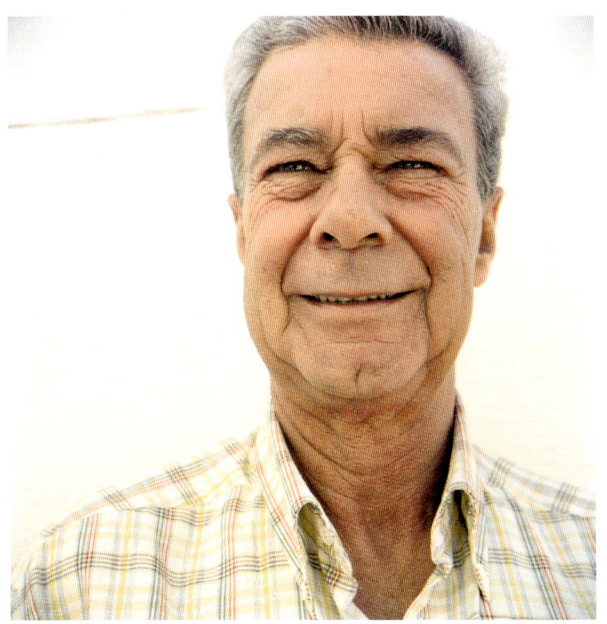

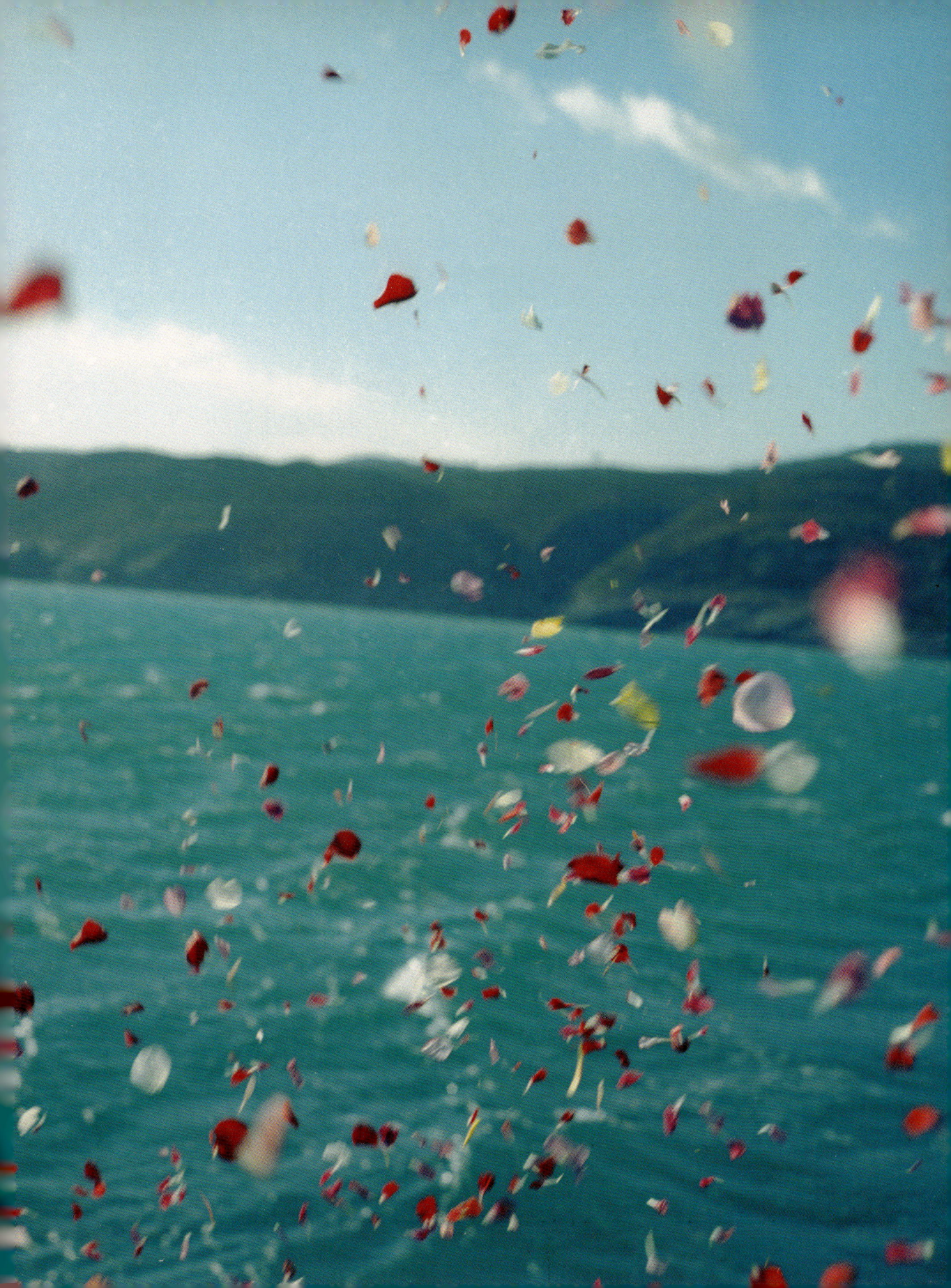

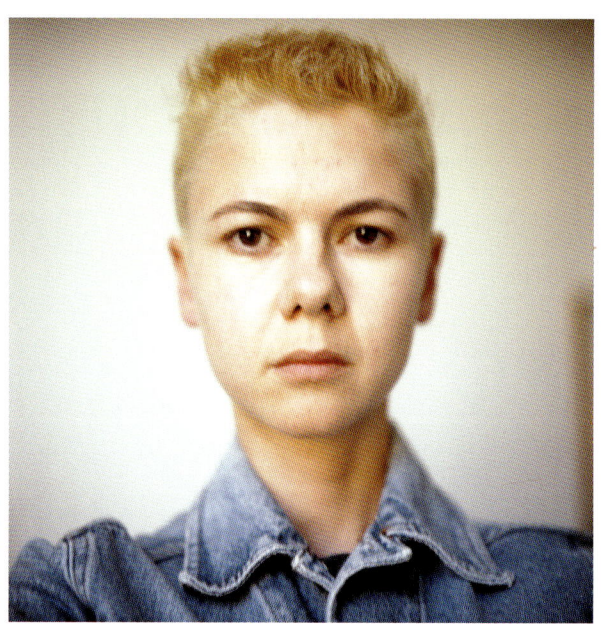

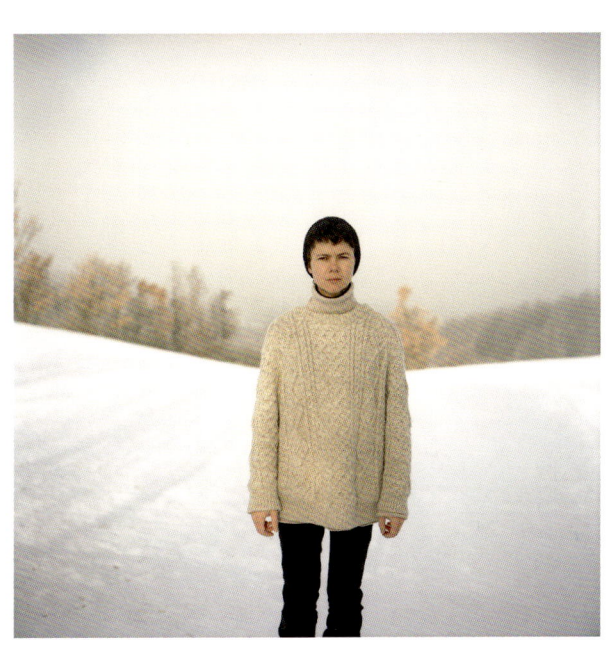

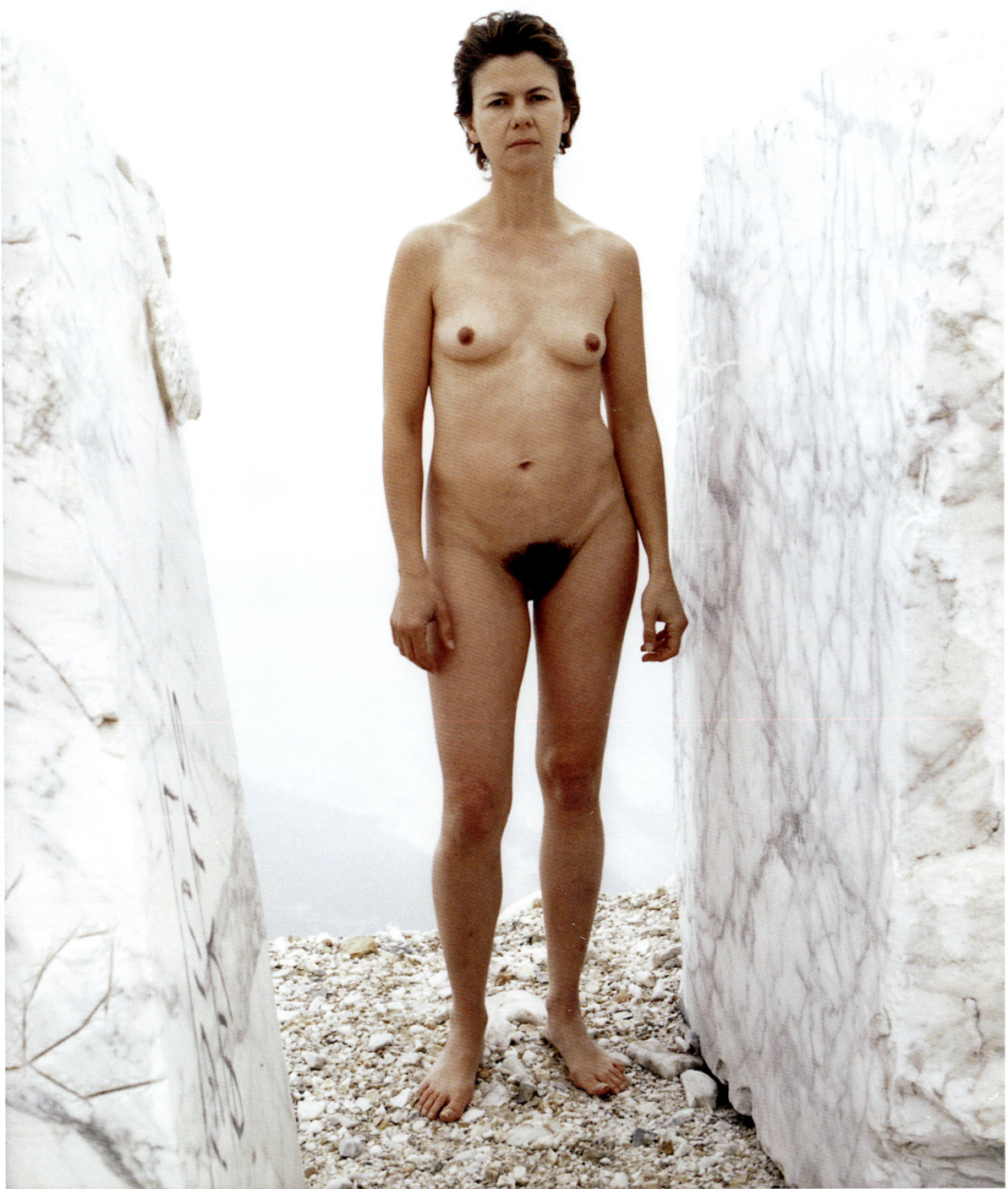

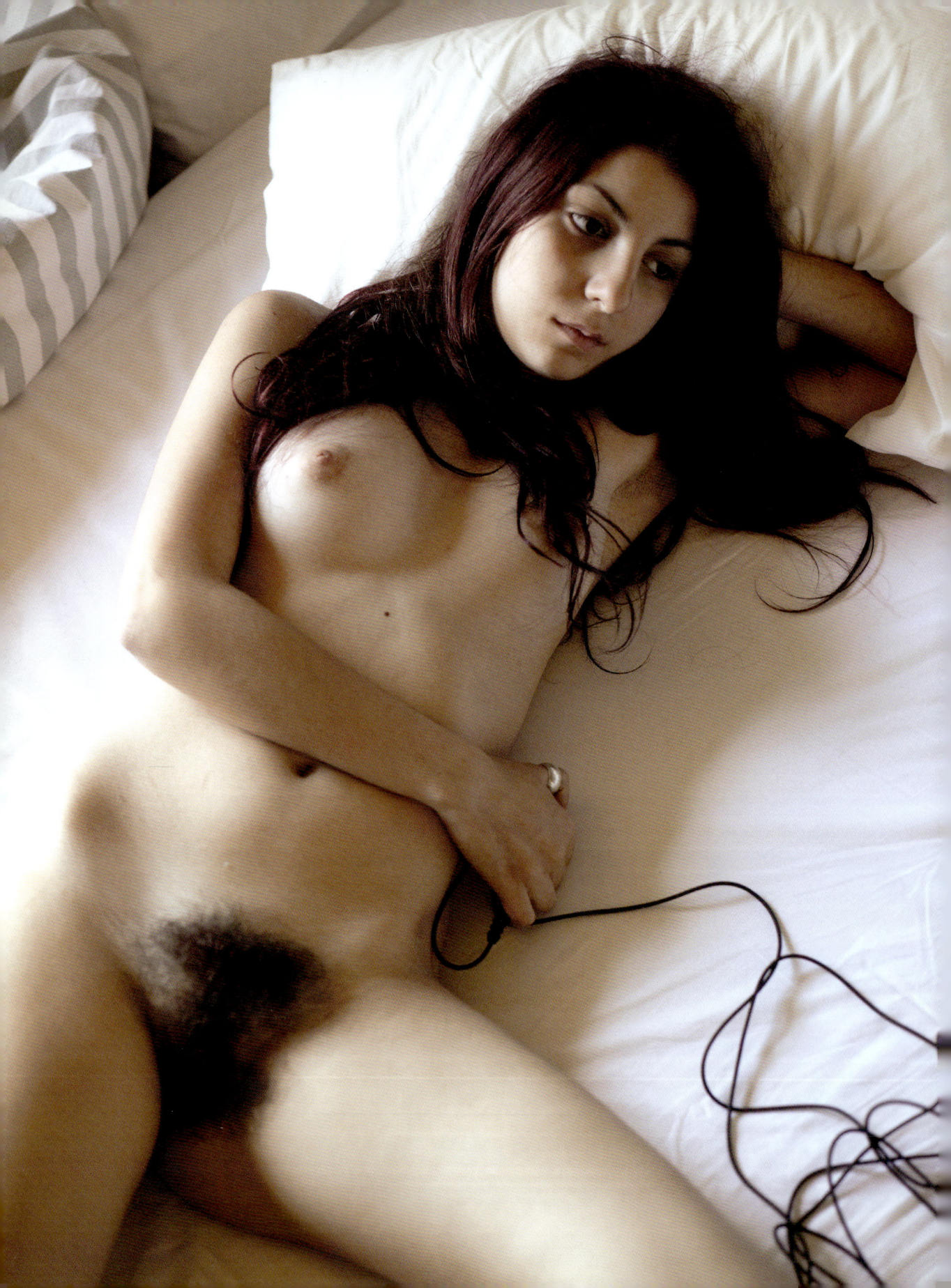

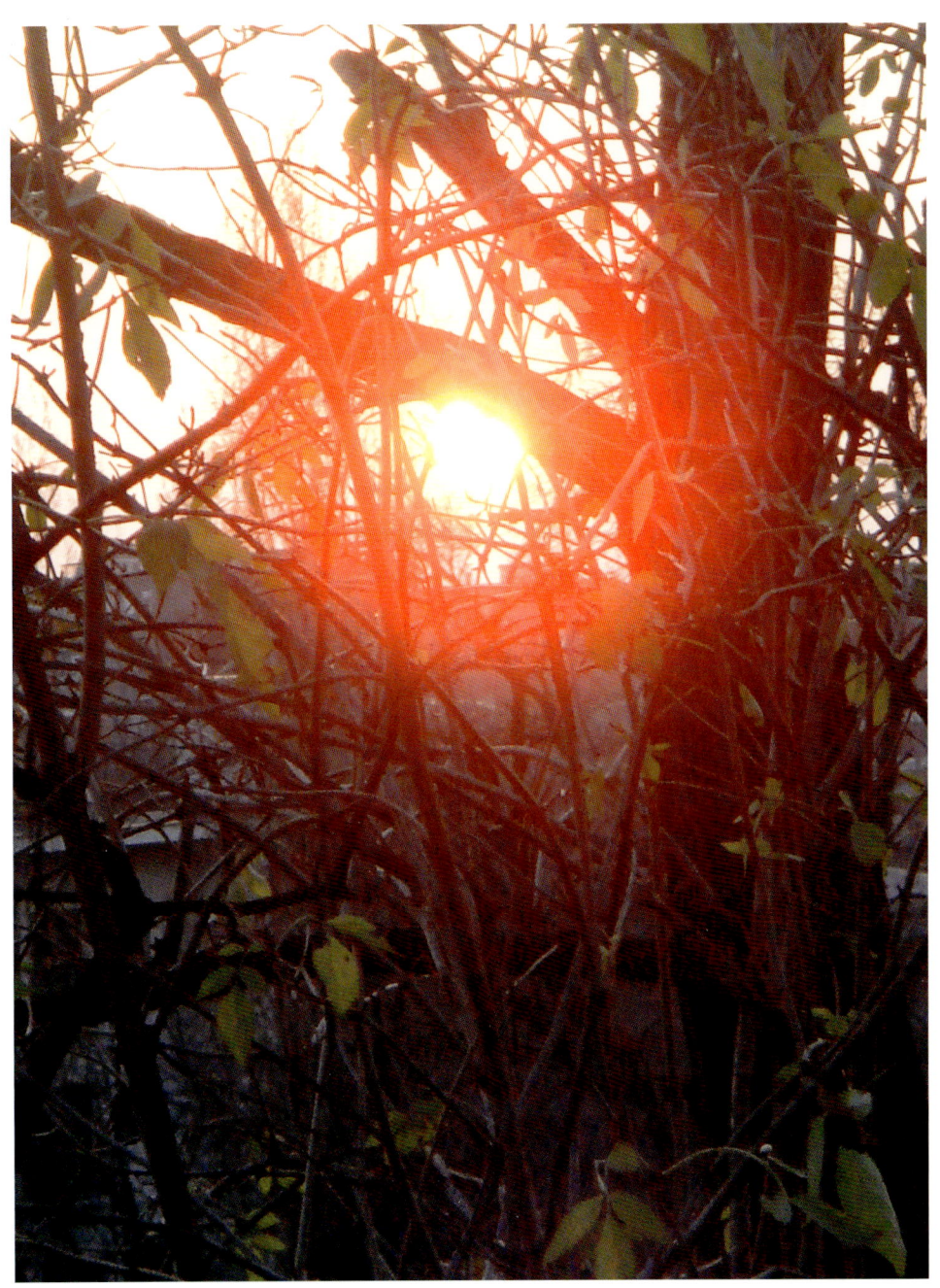

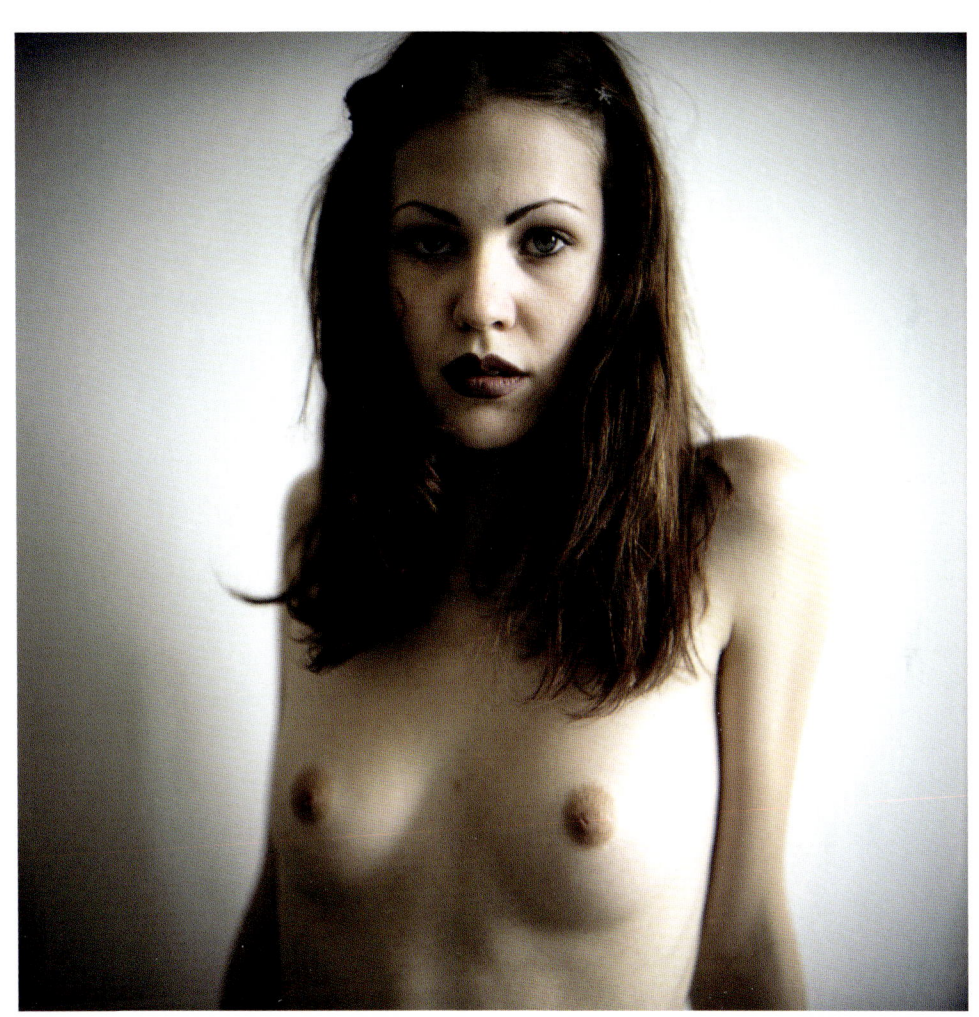

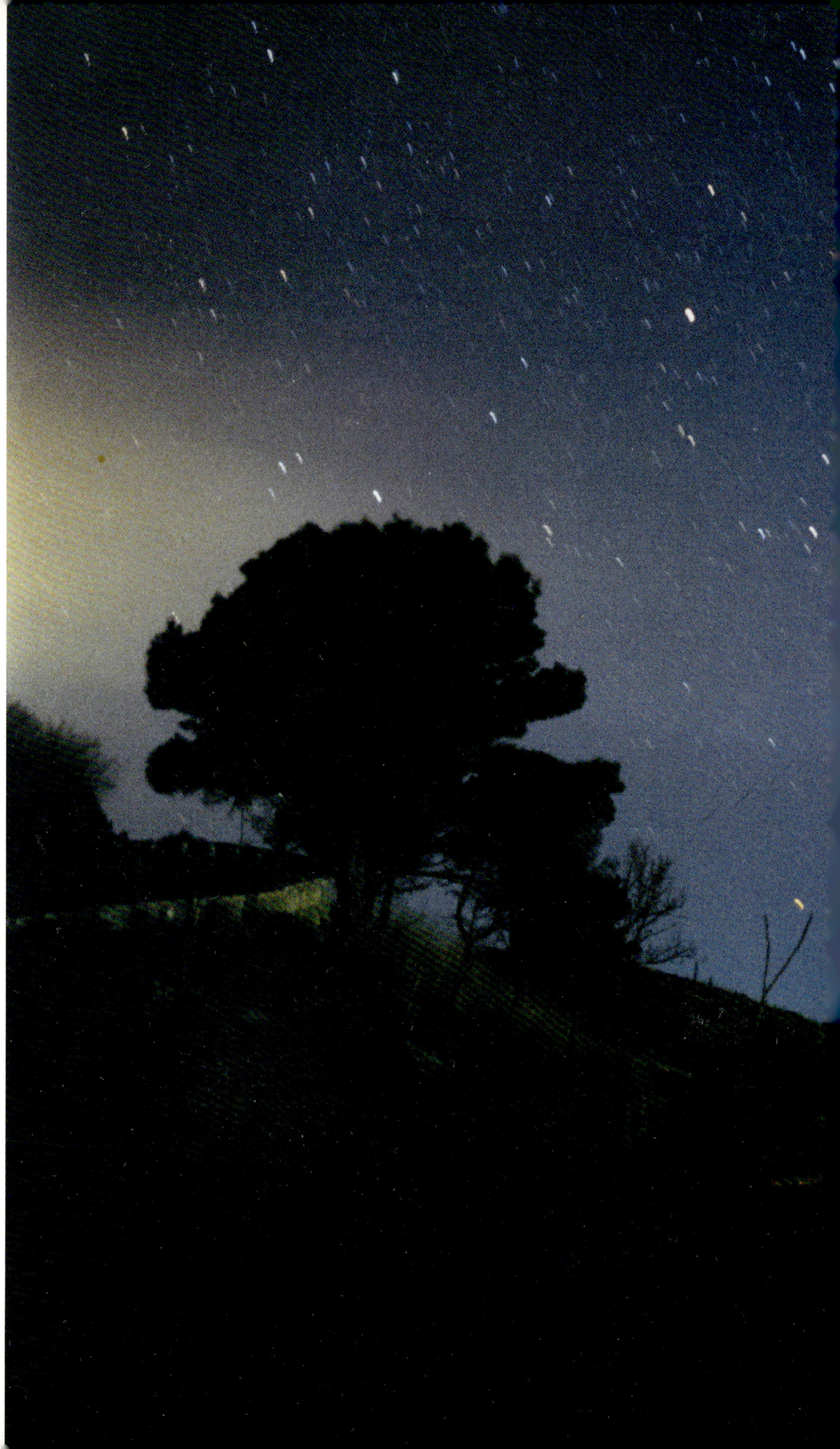

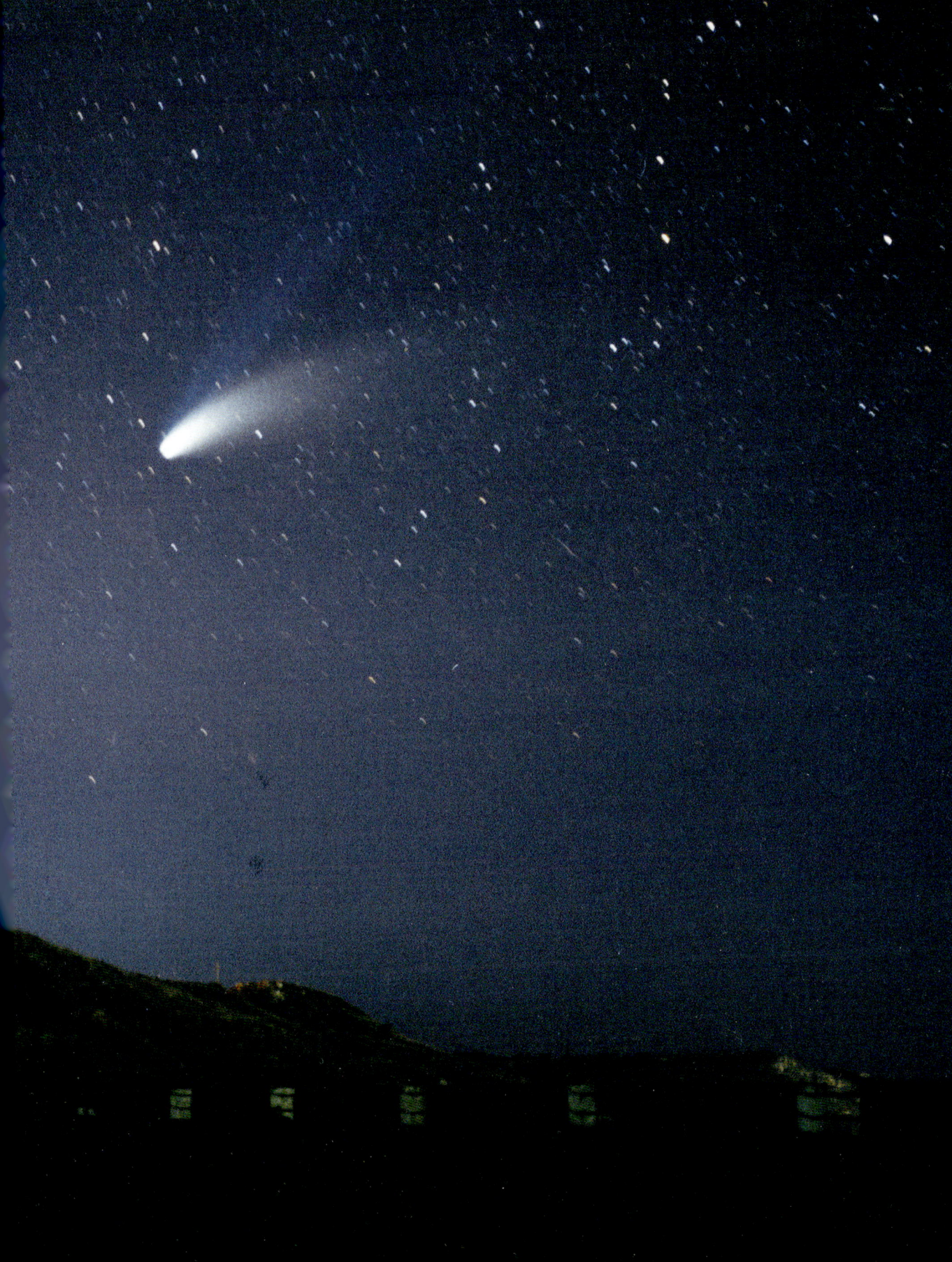

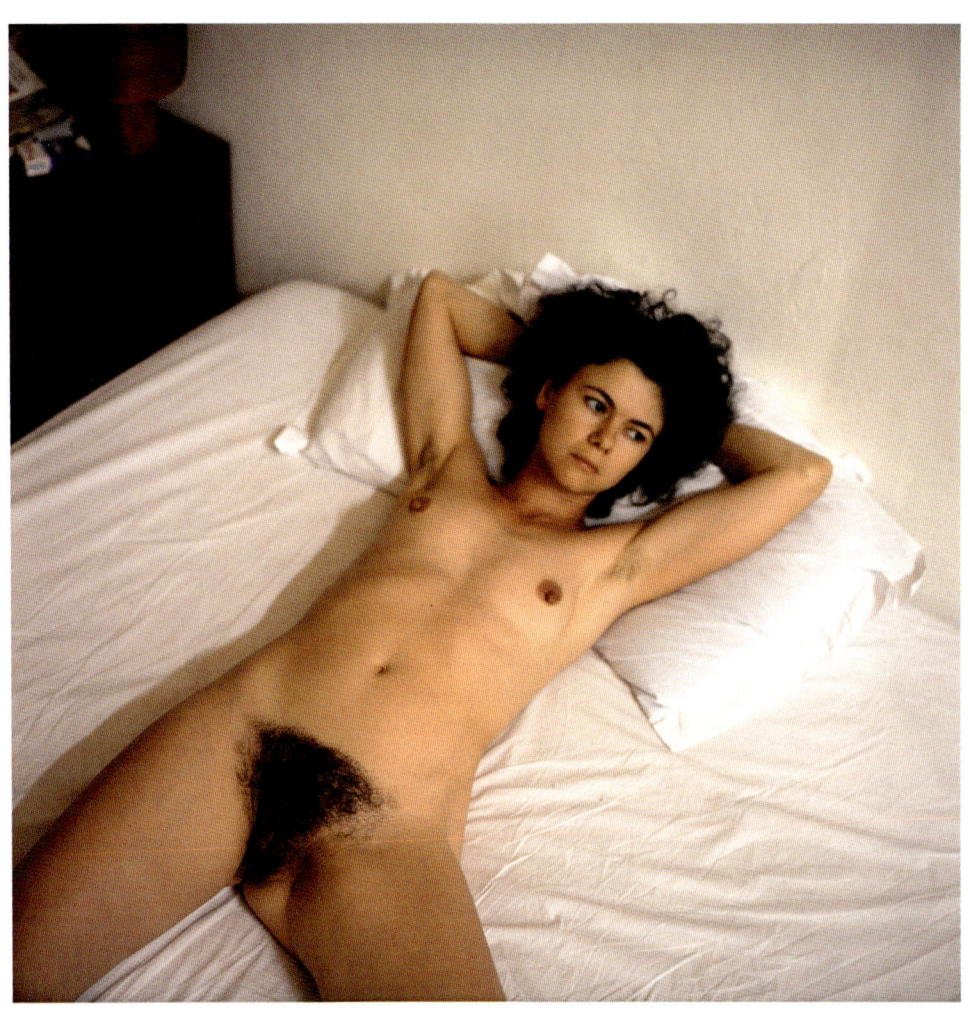

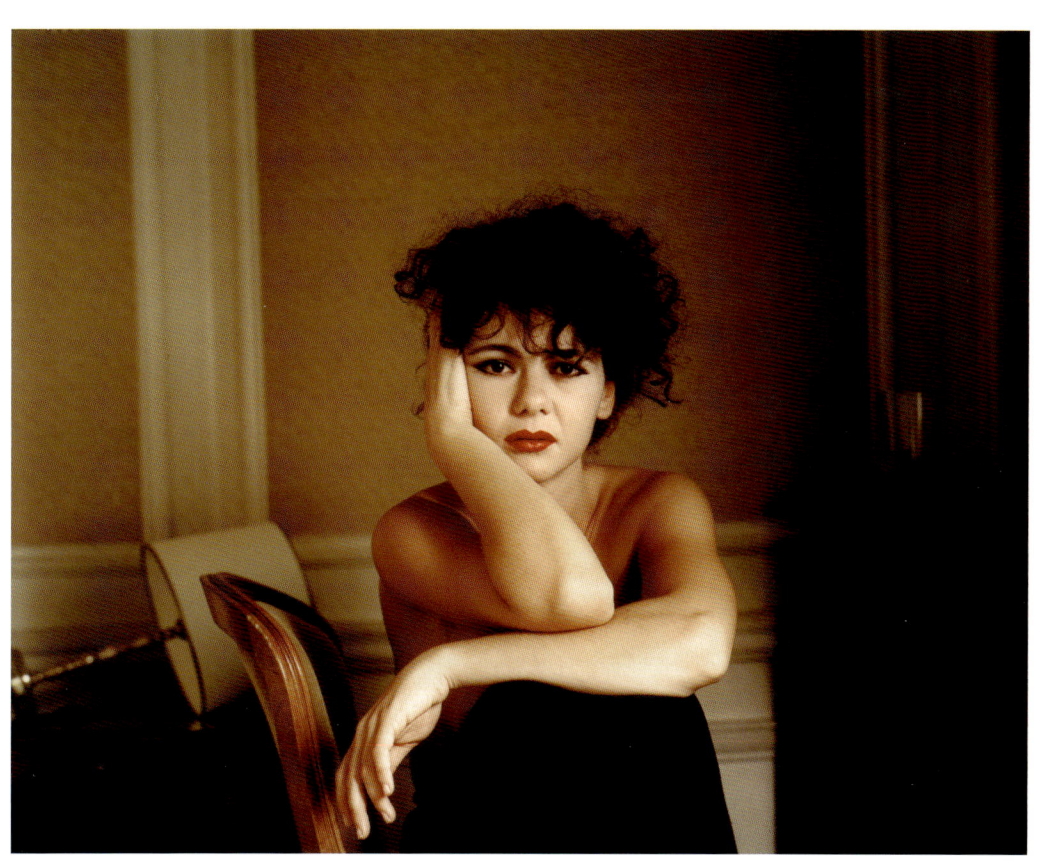

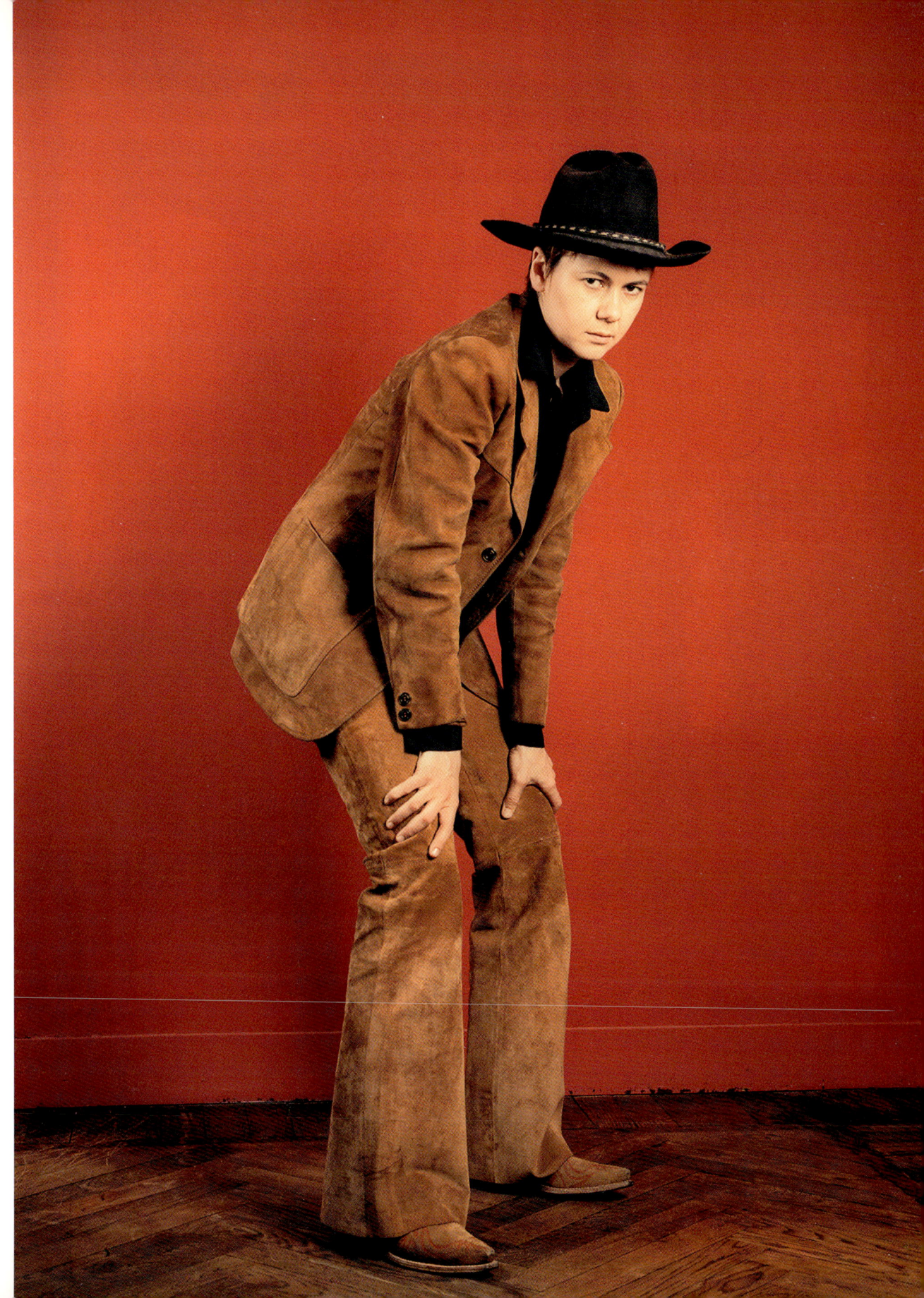

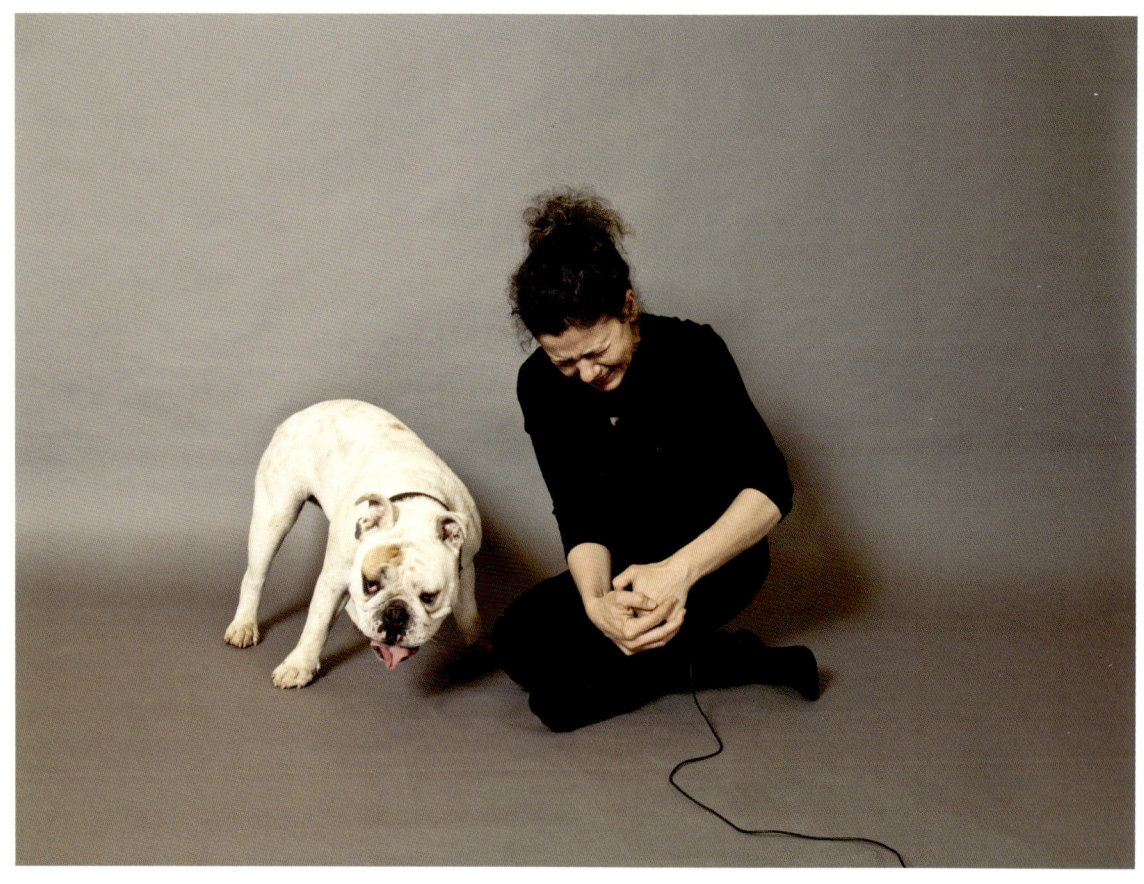

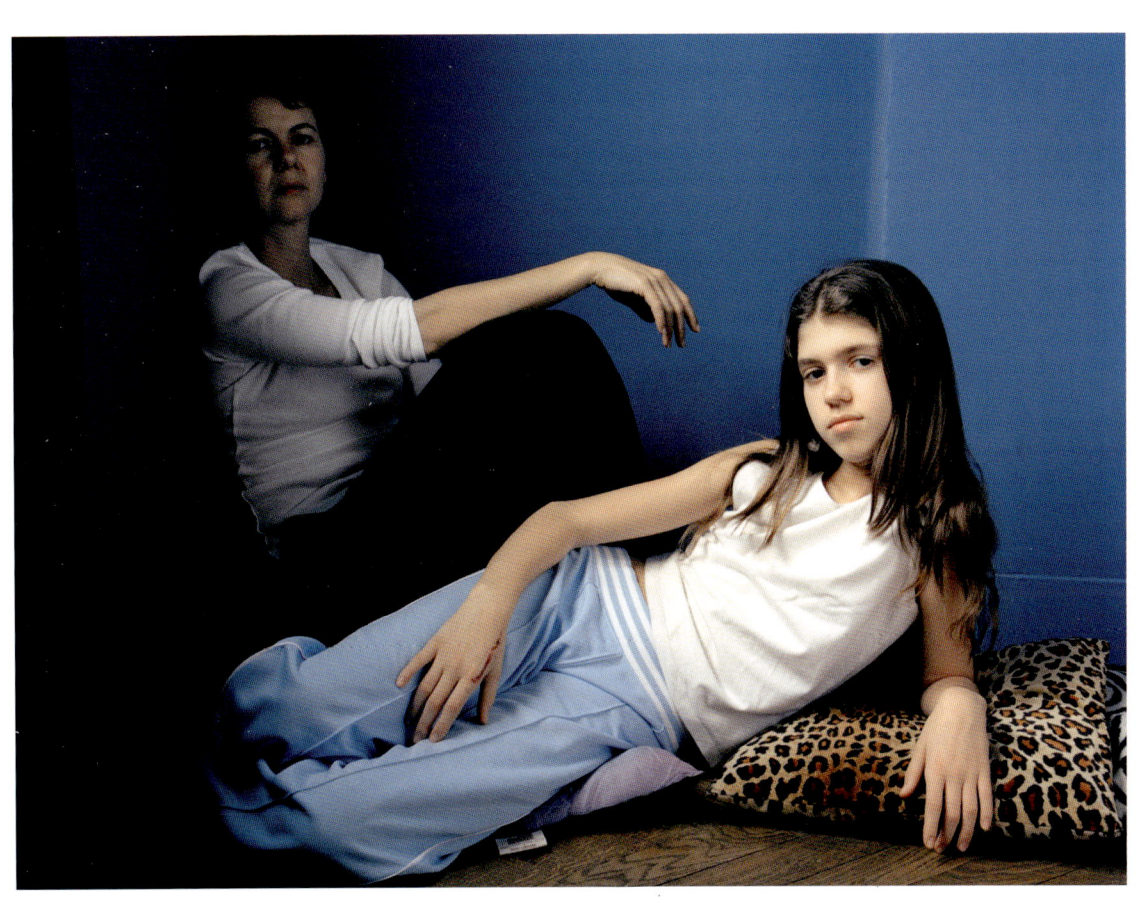

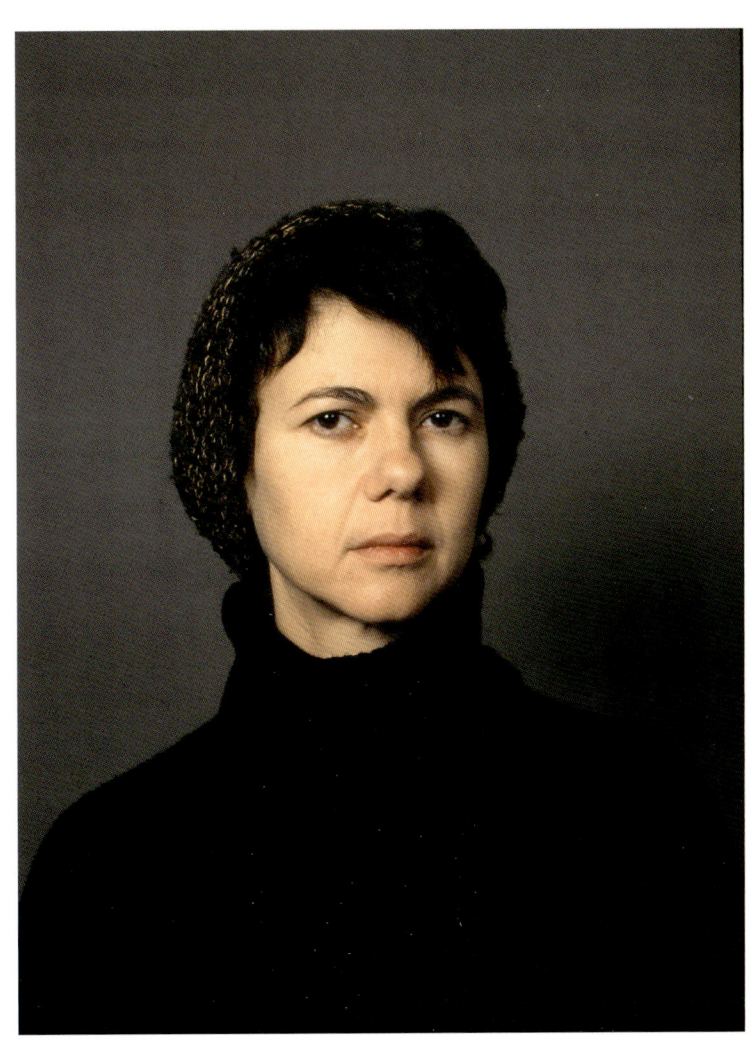

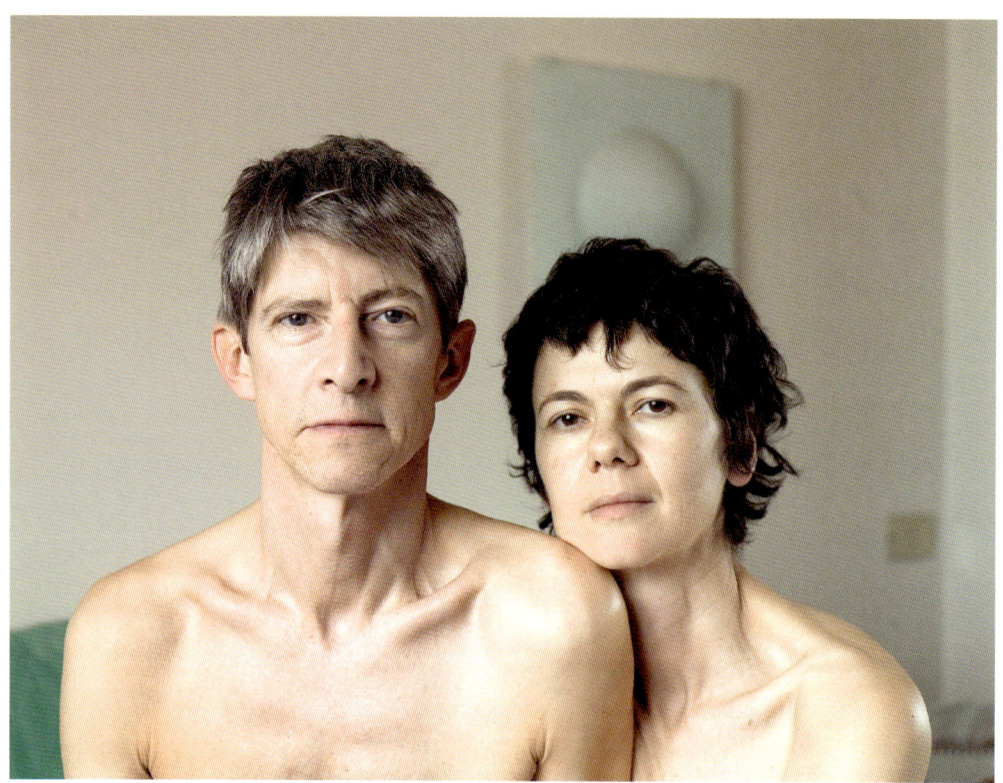

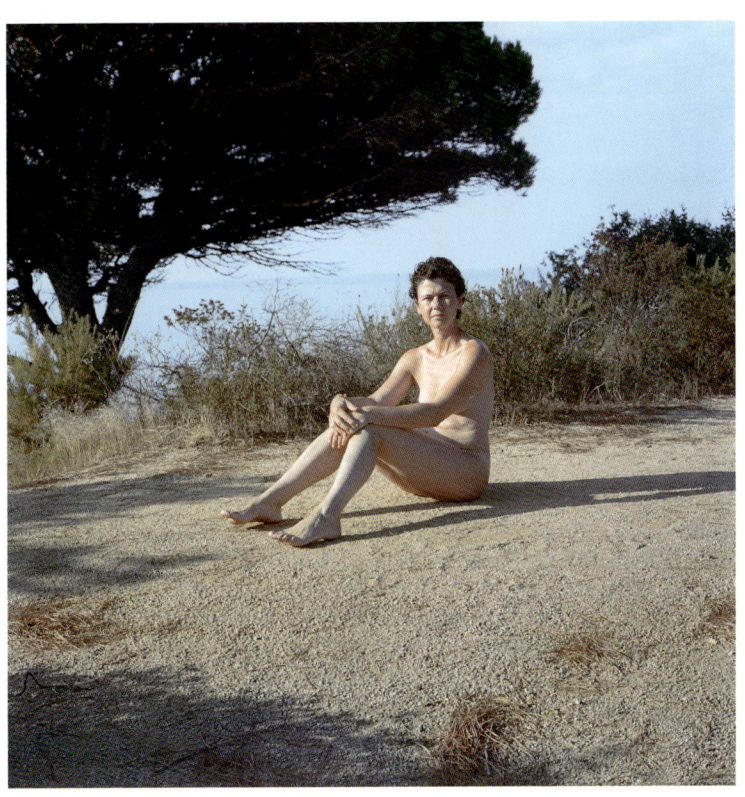

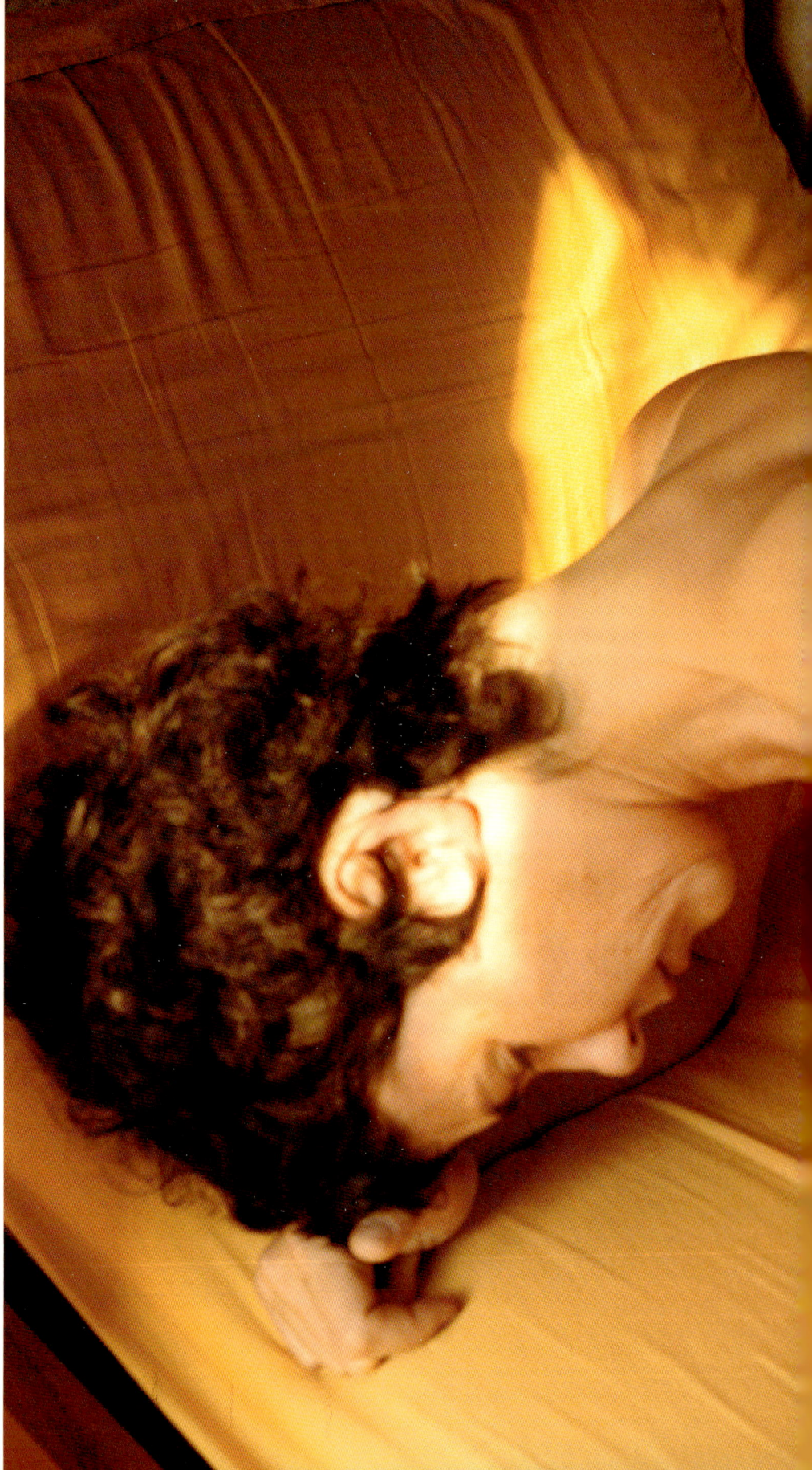

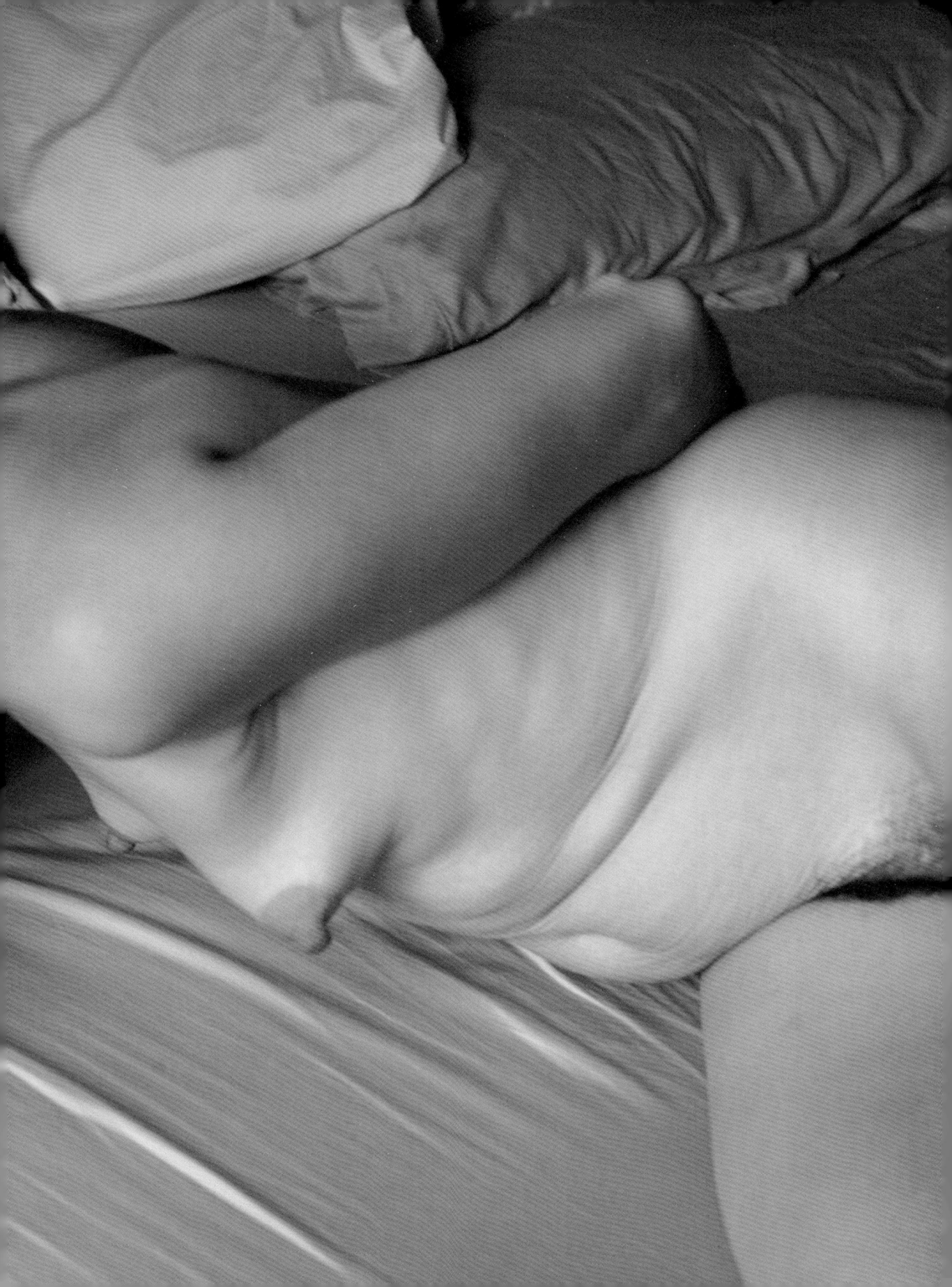

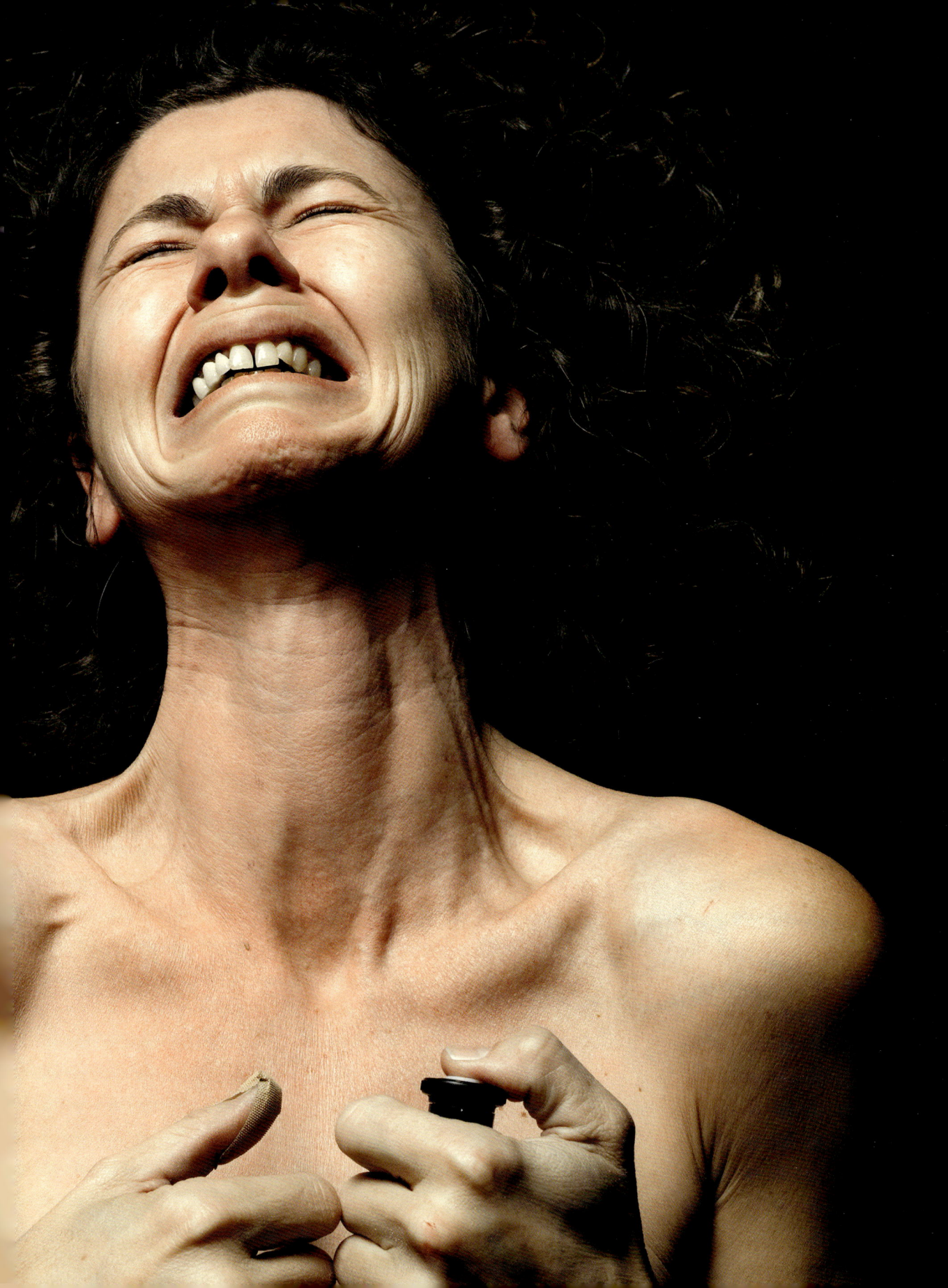

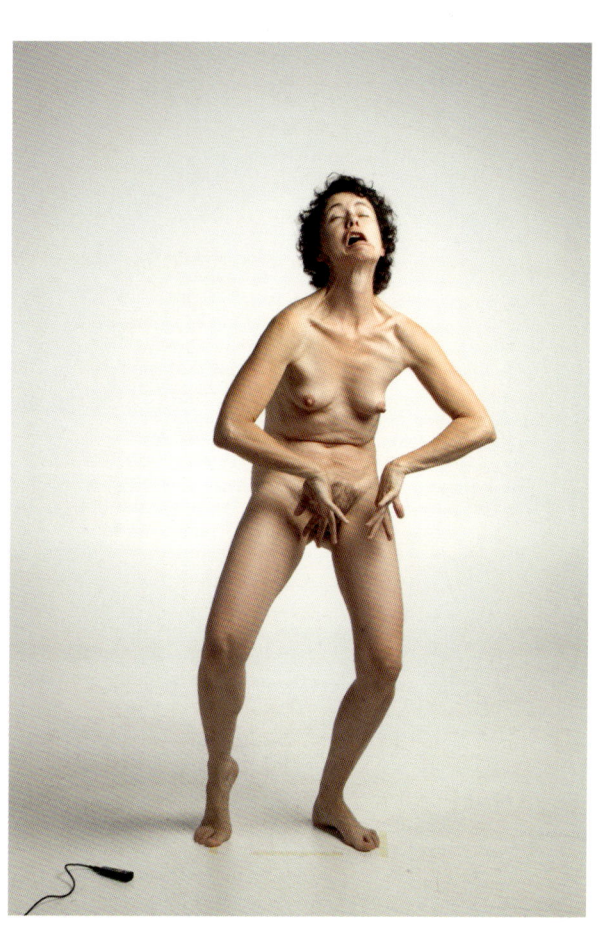

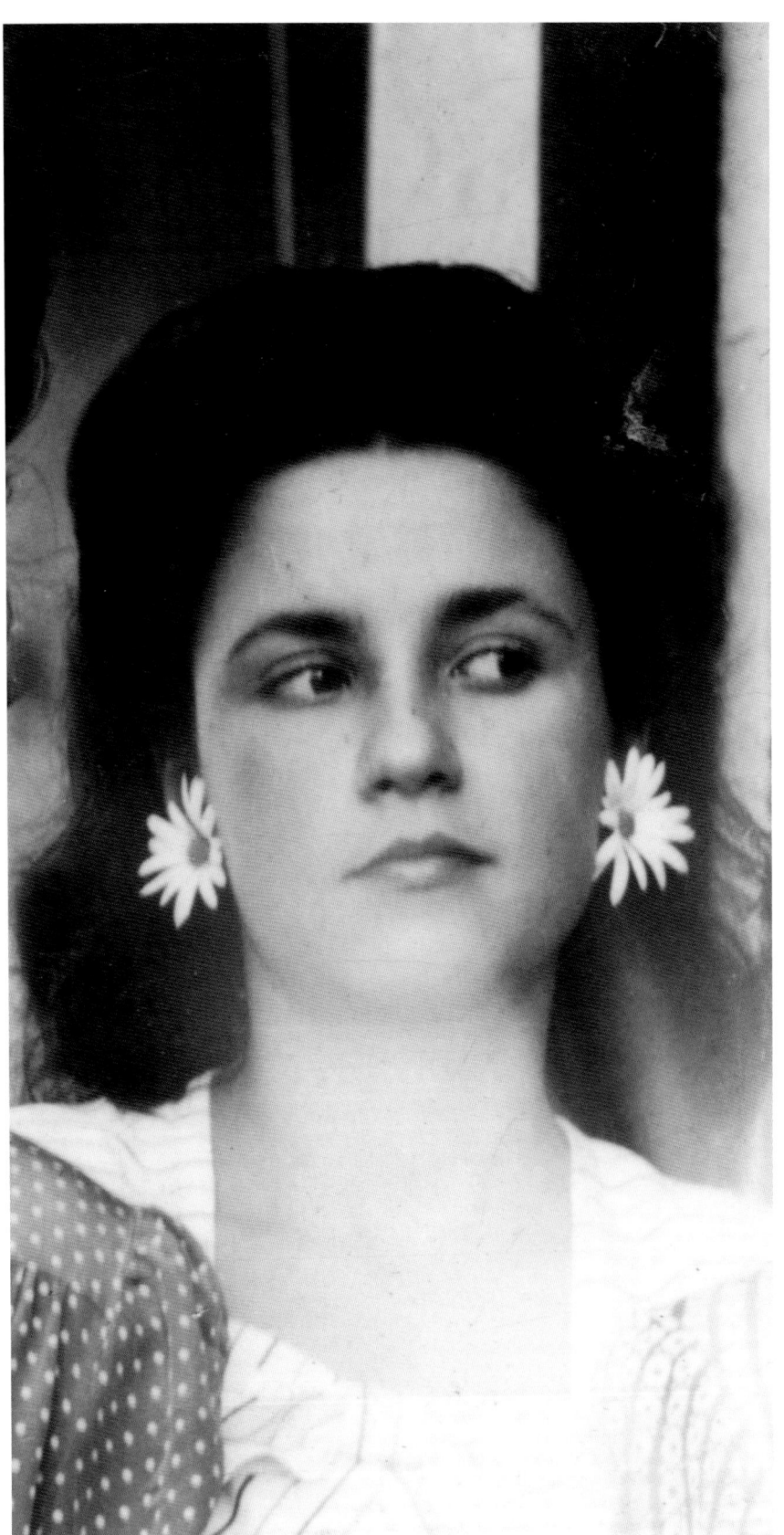

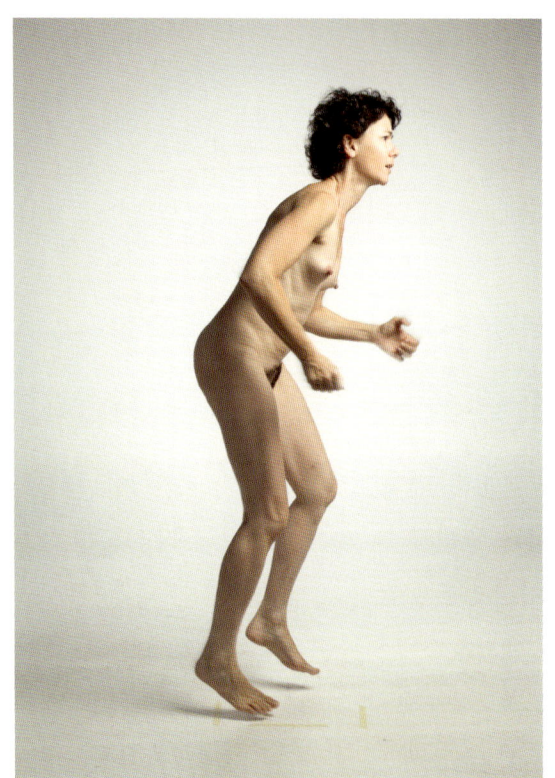

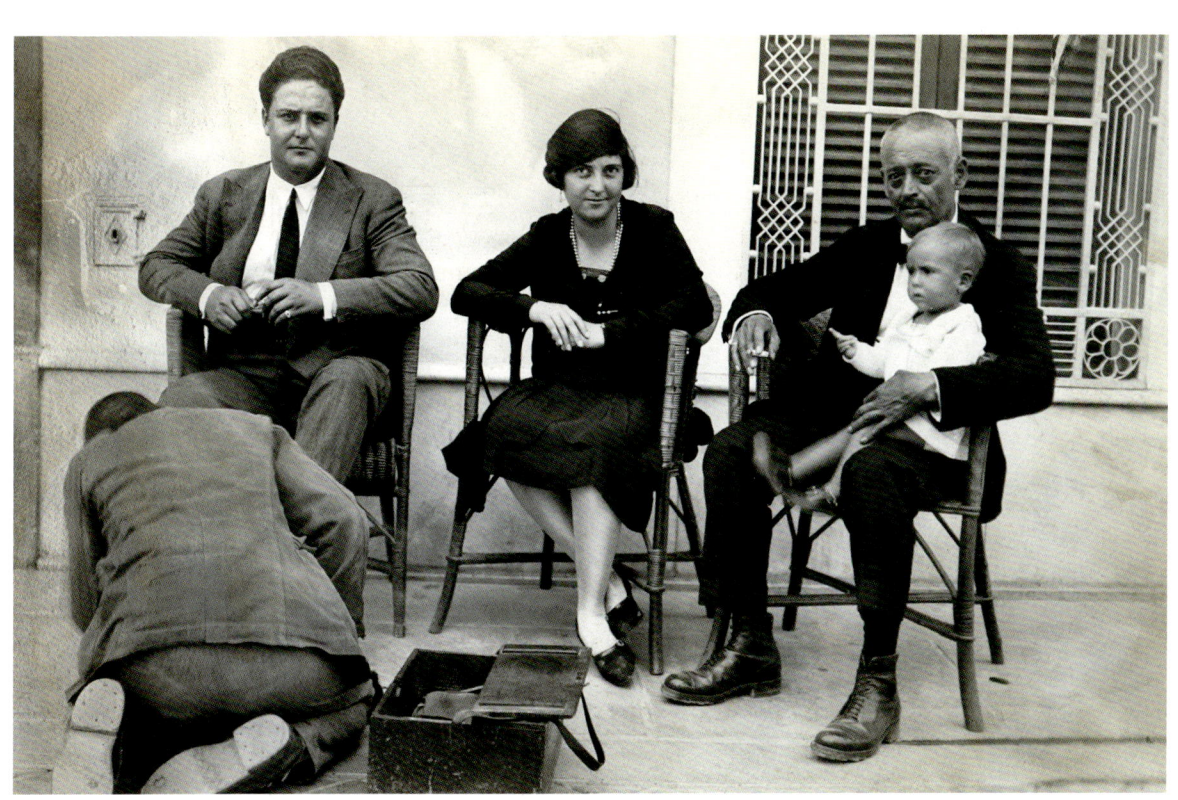

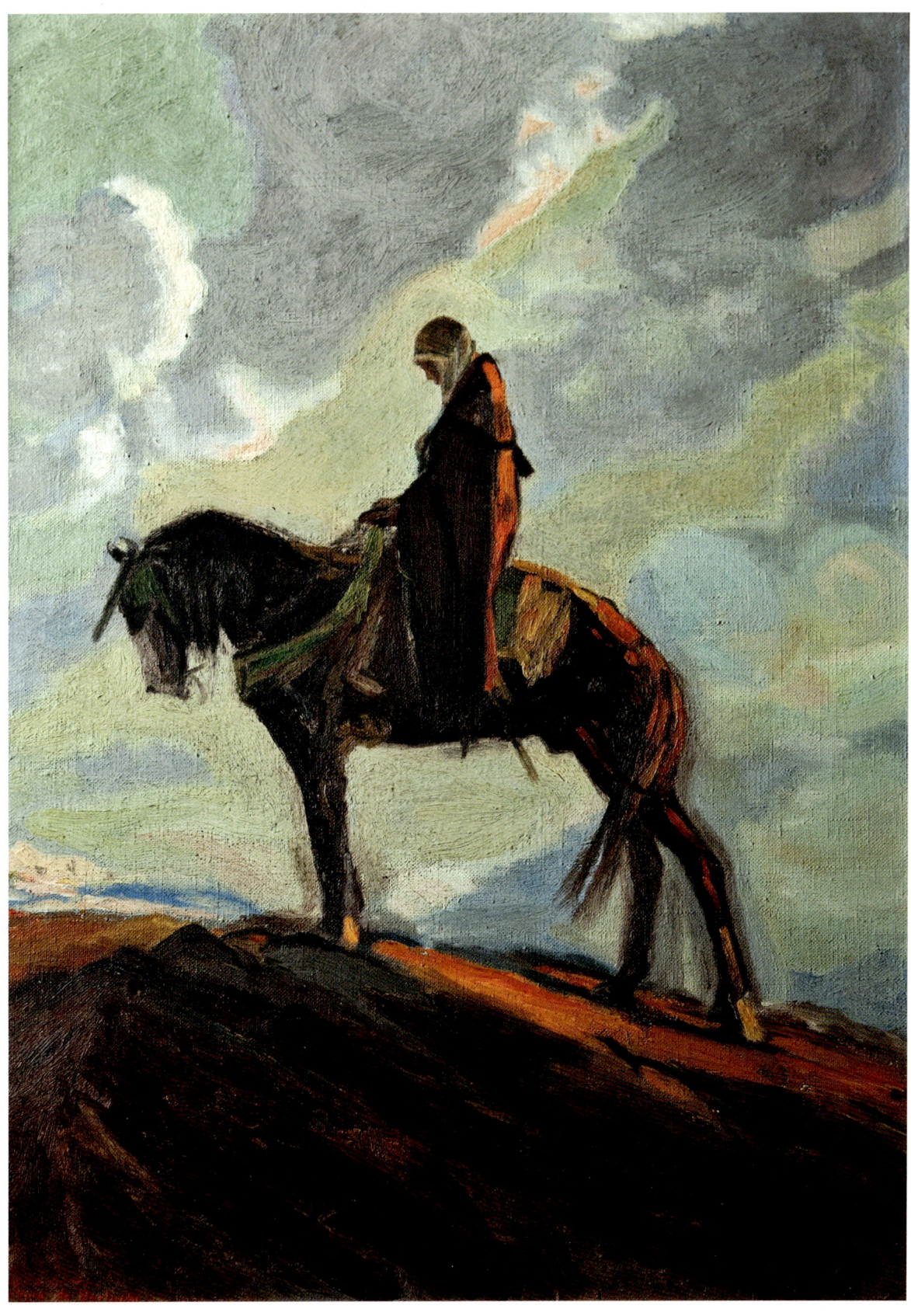

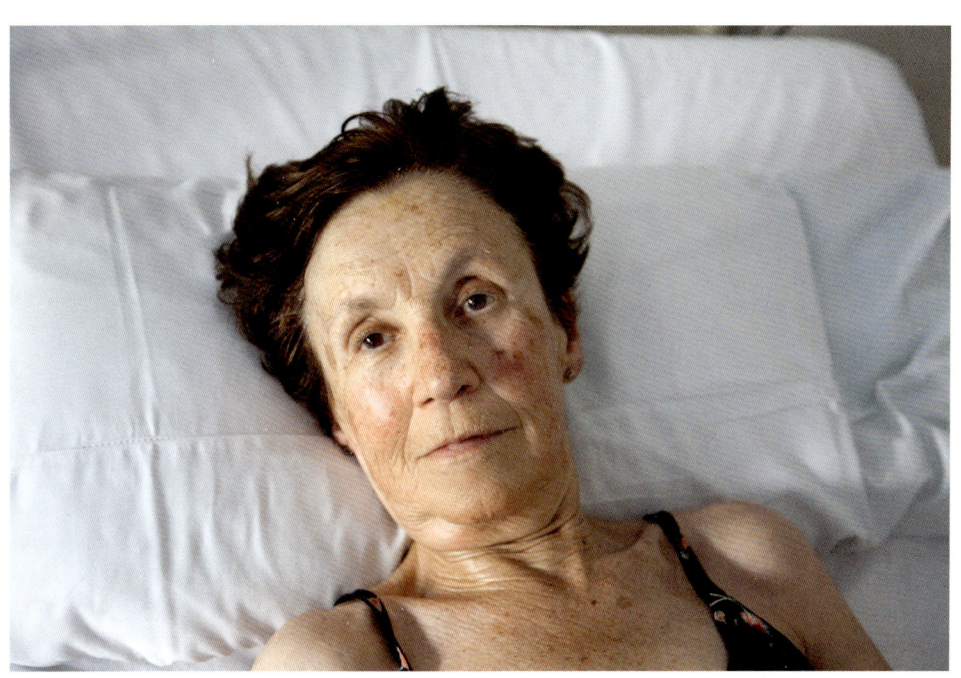

Photographs

Cover Barcelona, 1976. At 14 I wanted to be a model, so my sister Pati took a series of pictures of me. She processed and printed them, but eventually she didn't fix the print well enough, so it became yellow and many stains appeared.

Flyleaf Berja, 1925. My great grand-mother wrote letters in two directions.

p.2 Las Navas del Marqués, 1948. My father's family were high-rank officials in the Spanish Navy during Franco's dictatorship. My grandmother (a widow, dressed in black) appears here with Franco and his wife.

p.7 Madrid, 1946. My mother Maria Luisa (right) and her sisters Poli (center) and Uja (left). Only my mother married and had kids, but she had to abandon her career as an artist.

p.9 Milan, 2000.

p.10 Madrid, 1960. My uncle Momo wanted to be an artist, but when his father died of peritonitis in 1945, his uncle Edmundo forced him and his brothers to enroll in the Navy. Portrait of his daughter Ana, who led a very difficult life.

p.12 Cordoba, 1898. My great grand-father Manolo was the first car owner in Andalusia and opened the first Ford concessionary in Cordoba. He had this multiple portrait (called a Kintuplifoto) taken by Agustín Fragero.

p.12,13 Milan, 2004. My dancing self-portraits were taken during one of my worst depressions. I discovered that if I managed to express my despair in a picture, I felt much better.

p.14 Mauthausen, 1995. I took this self-portrait while I was working on my book To Hell and Back, about Jewish survivors to the Holocaust. I didn't know back then that we were Jewish, or that my great-uncle had collaborated with the German secret service during World War II.

p.15 Pontevedra, 1944. My uncle Pepe is one of the sailors in the picture, taken during his training at the academy.

p.16 Barcelona, 1974. I don't know who took this picture. I was 12, when my parents separated.

p.17 Dad on a boat by the sea, 1968.

p.19 Barcelona, 1988. I've always been in love with Dad. That's my husband's arm behind us.

p.21 Barcelona, 1980. I was already doing heroin here, but my face didn't show the drama yet. Photo by Manel Armengol

p.23 Barcelona, 1979. Fashion shoot.

p.24, 25 Barcelona, 1977. My boyfriend Nasi introduced me to the underworlds and we did heroin together for five years. He died of AIDS at 35, I survived. These images were taken by fashion designer Luis Fortes, a longtime friend.

p.27 Barcelona, 1982. My father once saw me walking down the street with a client. He sent me an ultimatum: he didn't want to see me anymore if I didn't stop drugs and prostitution. So one day I called my sister and asked her "Take me out of this hell". Photo by Antxon Gomez

p.28 Lublin, 1995. A large mausoleum in Majdanek brings together the ashes of millions of people exterminated in the camps in Poland.

p.31 Los Angeles, 1988. My very first self-portrait. I loved how my partner used the camera to portray people's inner life and strength, so I turned the lens to myself. I had found the way to re-create the gaze I needed so much.

p.32, 33 Zenica, 1998. I met a young boy from Bosnia. His name was Elvis. He had escaped the war. For the first time I could share my inner hell with someone else.

p.34 Gorazde, Bosnia, 1998. Elvis wrote me love letters from the Army.

p.35 Milan, 2007. My daughter Diana's self-portrait at 16, during my self-portrait workshop for teenagers. Diana was 3 when Elvis and I were lovers.

p.36 Milan, 2004. After coming back from Senegal, where she had spent 3 months with her dad, my daughter Yassine once asked me if she could take a self-portrait. She was 3 years old.

p.38, 39 Cadaqués, 1994 & 1998. After living the life he wanted, my dad died from a double cancer in his lungs and brain. We spread his ashes from a boat in his beloved Cadaqués.

p.40 Milan, 1998.

p.41 Borgotaro, 1998.

p.43 Carrara, 2004. Putting myself in extreme situations helped me to relieve my depression.
I took this "standing people" portrait at the marble quarries in February, it was -5°C.

p.44 Gorgonzola, 2009. Ylenia is one of Diana's friends, who participated in my workshop for teenagers. She took a collaborative self-portrait in my bed with my camera.

p.45 Milan, 2008. This image helped Olmo, another teenager who took part in that workshop, to let go of his burning rage.

p.47 Milan, 1994. I fell in love with Pola Weiss. When she left, I quit fashion photography.

p.48 Erice (Sicily), 1997. I photographed the Hale Bopp comet by chance, while I was working on my project "Heaven on Earth".

p.51 Milan, 1994.

p.53 Paris, 1986. My actress portrait was taken by my husband, while I was in an acting workshop with John Strasberg. I started pretending to cry, but then it came naturally.

p.55 Milan, 2004. I used to have a horse and I rode Western style. I love to be a cowboy. I often feel like a man.

p.56 Gorgonzola, 2009. In 2004, in a moment of deep distress, I abandoned my dog Nero. In 2009 I took a self-portrait with a borrowed dog, to work on my guilt and my loss.

p.57 Milan, 2004. The first picture with my daughter in which I was able to stay in the shadow and let her be the protagonist.

p.59 Milan, 2006. Alone again, after my relationship with Steve, and just before meeting Prem.

p.60 Milan, 2007. This self-portrait with Prem convinced me to get into a 30 year mortgage with him. We lived together in Gorgonzola for 3 years.

p.61 Tossa, 2004. Déjeuner sans herbe, sans rien.

p.62 Gorgonzola, 2008. I had seen my skin falling, and I wanted to capture that terrible vision, but I didn't manage.

p.64 Gorgonzola, 2008. I was going through the happiest and most peaceful moments of my life. But I was suspicious about happiness, so I started to study my difficult emotions. I wanted to claim my right to be desperate and still be loved and successful.

p.67 Turku, 2010. I was single again, and I felt ugly and unlovable, so I took horrible pictures of myself and published them. I knew that if I could see myself really ugly, I would become more free, and therefore, more beautiful. The evening of this photo-session a man seduced me on skype.

p.68 Madrid, 1946. Mum wearing homemade daisy earrings.

p.70 Turku, 2010. The importance of being ugly, uncool, vulnerable, ignorant, alone, poor, sick. I don't want a university degree. I don't read newspapers or watch TV. I want to remain ignorant of mundane things. I want to remain vulnerable.

p.71 Granada, 1928. My great grandfather Manolo with my grandmother Maria Luisa, her husband Gaspar, and my uncle Pepe on his lap, while the shoe cleaner was doing his job.

p.73 Maria Luisa Salmerón, "El suspiro del moro", 1947. My mother used to be an apprentice at Hidalgo de Caviedes studio in Madrid.

p.75 Barcelona, 2009. Mom's self-portrait after a stroke, at the hospital. She loved taking self-portraits, so I used my method to get close to her and accept the progression of her senile dementia. It's weird not to have parents anymore. In a way, I feel them both in me. I feel more emotionally stable, more secure, which is rather strange for me to say.

ACKNOWLEDGEMENTS

I want to thank, first of all, my family and ancestors, no matter how difficult our relationships have been. Without their influence, I wouldn't have become myself.

My mother, my father, my grandparents and great grandparents, my uncles and aunts, my sisters and cousins, and my two daughters.

I'd like to thank the men of my life, for all the love, the pain and the great life lessons; my friends and sitters who appear in this book, and the many friends who have inspired me and believed in my work, through the years. My heartfelt thanks to the known and unknown authors of the old photographs in this book; to my dogs and my horse.

A special thanks to Fabrice Wagner and Paul di Felice for making this book possible.

OSIC , the Bureau of Support to the Cultural Initiative of the Government of Catalunya.
The University of Luxembourg, FLSHASE, Laboratory for visual arts (IPSE).

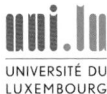 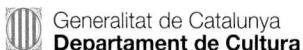

ISBN : 978-2-930537-20-7
Dépot légal : D/2012/10.458/7

www.caillolubleu.com
www.cristinanunez.com

Ce volume a été achevé d'imprimer en décembre 2012 sur les presses de l'imprimerie Newgoff à Mariakerke (Gent), Belgique

saludo ... pues yo tengo
... gradecesmos de vero por
... Te los ... manteleros
... lo que mejor se paresca
... vale poso que no del
el trabajo ... bueno
... Isabelita puede hacerse
Vasinos ... su primero para
... te quieres ... respeto
... Quiero que le hagan
... para que le ... menester
Blanco ... nigro que ... existe
... pues ... que se ...